CRUSHING IT ON STAGE

The Insider's Guide To Being A Successful Trainer

Fauzia Moorani

Crushing It On Stage:
The Insider's Guide To Being A Successful Trainer
Moorani, Fauzia

Copyright © 2019 by Fauzia Moorani

ISBN: 978-1-77277-291-3

No part of this publication may be reproduced, stored in a retrieval system or transmitted in any form or by any means, electronic, mechanical, photocopying, recording, scanning or otherwise.

All rights reserved, including the right to reproduce this book or portions thereof in any form whatsoever.

Published by:
10-10-10 Publishing
Markham, Ontario

First 10-10-10 Publishing paperback edition June 2019

Contents

Dedication	v
Foreword	vii
Acknowledgements	ix
Chapter 1: My Journey as a Trainer	1
Chapter 2: Trainers as Superheroes!	13
Chapter 3: I Could Never Do That!	25
Chapter 4: Oh No, I've Got to Do the Next Training!	37
Chapter 5: I'm Ready to Start. Now What?	51
Chapter 6: Ahhh! The Big Day Is Here!	69
Chapter 7: The E-Factor!	85
Chapter 8: No Budget? Are You Kidding?	97
Chapter 9: I'm So Glad It's Done, But How Did I Do?	105
Chapter 10: Hey, I Can Do This!	115
About the Author	125

I dedicate this book to all the females in my life who have shown me you can succeed at anything you want but still be true to yourself; and to the males who aren't afraid to stand behind us.

Foreword

Have you ever wondered what makes a trainer so successful? When planning your training sessions, do you wish you could be confident that it would go well? Do you want to strengthen your skills in front of an audience?

As I'm sure you know, not all trainers are great public speakers. You probably wish you had more insight from someone you could look up to. You are not alone! Yet, you probably have many skillsets that would make you a great trainer. You have made the right decision by picking up this book!

Fauzia Moorani will teach you everything you need to be a confident trainer. Her tips and strategies alone will ensure that your training is practical, relevant and successful!

In today's day and age, there are very few individuals who are prepared to share what makes them successful, with the intention to serve wholeheartedly. Fauzia helps you to see the potential that lies within you.

Crushing It On Stage

Get ready for an insightful journey, filled with humour, practical strategies, and moments of meaningful reflection. You'll be glad you picked up this book!

Raymond Aaron
New York Times Bestselling Author

Acknowledgements

"In everything we do, we must look to the future,
seeking always to think creatively,
to innovate and to improve."

Speech Extract from the Acceptance of the Charter of the Aga Khan University, His Highness the Aga Khan, Karachi, Pakistan, March 16, 1983

His Highness the Aga Khan works tirelessly for the betterment of society as a whole, inspiring us with his many qualities and hard work ethic. I am where I am, and who I am, because of his guidance, love, and inspiration. The above quote is a reminder that whatever I choose to do, it is important that I always seek to improve. Mediocrity is not acceptable. My hope is that this notion of constantly improving one's self resonates with you as you read this book.

I often get lost in the frantic day-to-day, something you may also relate to. Finding the time and space to be able to write this book was made so much easier with the constant support, encouragement, and patience (lots of it) of my husband, Shafiq, and two daughters, Jenna and Alysha. I could not have done this without their confidence in me!

My parents have always been role models in their passion and dedication to help others (in the family and in the community), for which my brothers and I have reaped the benefits. Throughout my life, I have always been able to count on my family (Hassam and Sunderji clan) for support, love, and of course, lots of crazy experiences that have given me material for my jokes! Thanks also to the Moorani clan for their encouragement and support; in particular, my brother-in-law, for his guidance and IT support (and I thought I was tech savvy)!

There have been many other individuals that have impacted me on this beautiful journey, for whom I am eternally grateful. A few kept me accountable, some showed me the impact of what I was doing, and others were excited to hear where I was in my journey! My sincere thanks to Nasrin; her endless support helped ensure that I was able to finish this book as quickly as I did.

In addition to my family and friends who have supported me throughout my journey, my life experiences have also shaped the person I am today, providing me with content for this book.

Although I loved working with students (shout out to the teachers from Ottawa who I had the pleasure to learn from

Acknowledgements

and work alongside), my work evolved to a stage where I was training adults.

I would be remiss if I didn't mention Zarina, who changed the trajectory of my life in ways I can't even explain. She brought me into the world of PTEP, as a teacher trainer, where I met remarkable educators and mentors from around the world, and had the opportunity to support scholars who exemplified what it means to be a truly passionate educator but with a gentle demeanor that is not always found.

My work at ITREB Canada (as a Professional Teacher Educator, and eventually as a Training and Development Lead) has definitely impacted my growth as a trainer. Right from the start, I was mentored by individuals who nurtured and empowered my colleagues and me, to be successful in our role. There were several who have been with me from the start as a PTE, as well as those I met along the way (the whole PTE team, as well as my current team; not just colleagues but truly wonderful human beings that I will always feel connected to), in addition to the STEP teachers who I had the pleasure to work alongside and learn from. The drive, commitment, and care from these teams is a true inspiration.

Recently, I worked with a team of passionate and energetic educators at LEARNstyle, who use technology as a tool for students with exceptional needs. Through them, I strengthened my computer skills, as well as reignited my passion for working with students.

While completing the Adult Learning and Development Program, I had the opportunity to see fantastic trainers (in particular, Pauline, Josie, and Josh) who helped me grow as a facilitator, as well as learn from colleagues who were driven and passionate. My exposure to great speakers continued with the Cambridge Assessment International Education team (Lorna, Ray, Judith and Paul) who truly demonstrated their love for educational leadership, and whom I had the privilege to work alongside and learn from (in addition to the team from the IIS).

Not too long ago, I took a chance and went to a session held by Raymond Aaron and James McNeil. You see, I had always wanted to write a book, but it wasn't until I met them that I knew I had it in me. Through them, it became a reality, and for that, I am forever thankful. I also met some wonderful individuals who were on this journey with me, and look forward to their continued success in writing their books.

Lastly, but by no means the least, I would like to take a moment to thank you for picking up this book. I hope it provides you with comfort, confidence, and a bagful of practical strategies that you can implement in your journey. If you laugh along the way (or even smile), then all the better!

Chapter 1

My Journey as a Trainer – What Was I Thinking?

You picked up this book and have me curious! Why? What was it that made you do it? Perhaps it was because you know me, and you were thinking, "Does she actually know how to write a book?" Or perhaps you are a family member that felt obligated to buy it! Some of you may actually be interested in the topic, and want to try to be a better public speaker or a trainer. Regardless of why you chose to do this, I am glad to have you be a part of this journey, and that is what this truly is! I'm going to start off by sharing my journey and how I got here! Why? You'll find out soon enough!

People often say to me that I was born to be a public speaker, and that it comes naturally to me. Boy, if they only knew! As a child, I was very quiet at home; maybe because my brothers and cousins were the loud and talkative ones! I'm not sure why it was like this, but it just was. At school, I was also shy. I would be afraid to raise my hand and give answers. I would never go out of my way to talk out loud. For those of you who know me, you are probably saying, "No way! I don't believe it!" But it's true!

It wasn't until I was with my friends that I would act crazy. Literally! I was what you would call the class clown! I loved making my friends laugh. I think I thrived on it. We could hang out for hours, and I would entertain them with my crazy jokes and my silly comments. I did have a serious side, but this goofy side was definitely one that stood out. Some of you who know me may be thinking, "So not much has changed since you were a kid!" Ah, but I still continued to be shy when in front of a crowd of people. I remember one of my teachers saying, "Still waters run deep!" when they were referring to me. It took me a while to figure that one out!

Today, I still have that goofy persona, but I'd like to think that I use it for good. What do I mean by that? Well, I find that this side of me allows me to connect with people and build a relationship with them. People see me as approachable, and this impacts everything that I do. You will see, in later chapters, how this can be advantageous as a trainer. Hmmm, for those of you who don't share this crazy gene, you may be wondering if this book is for you! Don't worry, you don't have to be exactly like me to succeed. In this book, I share many of my secrets to becoming a successful trainer. One of those is about being yourself! But back to the idea about being successful. What does that mean exactly? It may mean different things to different people. For me, it means that you enjoy what you do, and you know you are making an impact. How do you know? We'll talk about that later in another chapter!

When did I decide to become a trainer? It was a long and crazy journey for sure. I remember when I was at university, studying in a program that I wasn't sure I really wanted to be in. I was in one of my classes, and the task was to get in front of the class and convince the audience to do something. There I was, sitting in front of my peers, sharing my story about a close family member who was very ill. I got quite emotional as I spoke to them about how I was witnessing my family member's health slowly deteriorating right in front of my own eyes. At the end, I asked them to donate some money to my cause, which would not help my loved one but could hopefully help others find a cure. When I finished the presentation, I was approached by several of my peers who were ready to donate. I had to explain to them that I made up the story, to which they were not very happy! Look, in my defence, it was an assignment. I wasn't purposely trying to deceive them! Their reactions aside, I think it was at that moment that I truly felt the power of the stage. (Perhaps a career in acting would have been lucrative.) It can be so empowering to be up there, knowing you can impact the audience—hopefully, in a good way!

Despite this realization, I kept going on with my education, trying to find a career that truly made me feel whole. Unfortunately, I was also dealing with a lot of personal issues at that time. My life had taken a turn as I was dealing with a relationship that wasn't going well. I began to feel less and less confident in who I was and what I could achieve. Had it not been for the support of my family and close friends, I am not sure where I would be today. I needed to believe in myself again, and after trying several different programs, I ended up in teacher's college. It was a whirlwind but an exciting one. I was finally out there, in front of an audience, albeit with 32 screaming kids who didn't always listen when you told them what to do. I was truly lucky though, as I had several mentors and colleagues that made it a great experience. Not to forget the students, I learned from them almost as much as they did from me. (At least I hope that they learned from me!) But as much as I loved it, there was too much turmoil in my life at that time, and it took a toll on me. After about 5 years, I was given an opportunity to leave the classroom and enter the world of training. It was the best decision I ever made—

not that I really hated the classroom, but I was already feeling burned out!

Training others opened a whole new world for me. I participated in a teacher training program, of which some of my mentors were outstanding, and some left something to be desired. I mean, why would you train the audience about the art of teaching, and not use any of the strategies to do it? Really? How does that even make sense? And so, my learnings began.

After my own training, I started providing professional development for others. It truly consumed me! I loved working with these teachers. I was also learning along the way, and my confidence started to rise. Admittedly, there were good moments, and then there were some tough ones. I remember one day in particular. I was leading a session for a group of educators—and remember how I told you I had that goofy side to me? Well, I like to crack jokes in my sessions, as I find that it makes it more engaging, and it lightens the mood. On that day, I made a joke and tagged a teacher in the comment. It was more like a tease. Everyone laughed (including the teacher; at least I thought she did), and we moved on to the next topic. At the end of the day, we were all eating lunch, and as I was walking toward the food line, the same teacher who I had teased jokingly, approached me. I can't remember her exact words, but I still remember exactly how she looked at me. She told me that after the session, she started to cry. How dare I make fun of her like that? I was honestly shell shocked! What was she talking about? I wasn't serious. I was just trying to lighten the mood and had made a joke. Unfortunately, she felt it was at her expense. Why am I telling you this? I literally took this with me everywhere I went. For the next few months, it was all I could think about. I couldn't believe how reckless I had been, just to get a laugh. It was a life lesson for me, and something I try to keep in my mind every time I am doing any kind of training. I know you can't please everyone; along the way, there will be times when people won't agree with what I do or how I frame things. I have no control over that, but what I do have control over is how I react to this information, and how I use it as a learning for the future.

Becoming a trainer was a blessing that opened all kinds of doors and experiences for me. I was now introduced to great facilitators, for my own professional development, which was key to my role. After all, if I don't grow as a trainer, how can others grow in my presence? I'm not trying to say that everything revolves around me. It doesn't. But through my role, I was able to provide opportunities for others to grow as educators, in addition to growing myself. I have had the pleasure of seeing some great teachers in action, and that meant I was able to share these lessons during my training sessions. The other thing that was key, was that I made note of what worked well for me and what I struggled with. In fact, I was at a training session recently, where the facilitator often went off on tangents. Boy, did I get irritated! Did I want to know about how his mother used to clip his toenails, even when he was an adult? Okay, so that wasn't what he shared, but believe me when I say that he was totally off topic! I am sure you can also think of a session that you attended where that happened. How did it make you feel? I felt like the trainer wasn't valuing and being respectful of my time. Maybe you felt the same way. Again, another learning that has impacted me when doing my own sessions.

I remember, one time, going out of town for some professional development for my work. It was a great experience; after all, I got to hang out with my colleagues (many of which had become good friends) in an exciting city. However, the sessions left a lot to be desired. They seemed completely unrelated to what I was doing in my role. I didn't understand why I had to attend them, and I know I wasn't the only one who felt that way. At one point, one of us raised it with our supervisor. Her reply has always stuck with me. She said that in every session there is a gem you can walk away with. You just need to be open to receive that gem. This particular learning has stayed with me for life; so yes, I try to remember that every time I am at a training session! This notion of intellectual humility is one that is essential for any educator. As a trainer, it is important that you are constantly open to learning.

I often get asked why I have kept working as a trainer. Well, to be honest, there were definitely times when I wanted to quit. One particular reason for that was the lack of work-life balance. Why? Well, admittedly, I became a workaholic. You know that idiom, *eat, sleep, breathe?* Well, that's what I did about work. It was on my mind non-stop! Partially because there was always so much work to do (and definitely not enough manpower), but also because I loved the work. I loved how it felt to create resources for others to use, and to prepare presentations for training, but also the feeling of doing the training itself! It gave me this *high*, without the drugs! When I walked in the room to do a session, or got on a webinar to train online, I felt energized! Don't get me wrong; I felt nervous, but in a good way! It was almost like I harnessed this feeling, so it flowed through me, like it was nourishing my soul while I was there. What? I know it sounds somewhat crazy. Okay, it sounds really crazy! The only way I can explain it is by saying that I felt energized to my core; that I had been given a purpose, and that was what I was there to do. In fact, right before I would do a training session, I would say in my mind, *"Help me to serve you."* There I go again, talking to myself! Seriously though, I feel like I am here to serve, and for that reason, anything I do, I give it my all. This notion of service is one that I feel strongly about. I truly believe that we are all here with a purpose. I don't know if this is mine, but it sure feels like it is an important part of who I am.

By this point, you are probably beginning to think that this woman is either from a cult or just crazy. Funny, but not true. I just believed that if people were going to give up their time to come to one of my training sessions, then it was important for me to give it my all. I needed to be fully present, to ensure that I did my best to achieve the outcomes I had set for myself. Yes, there were times when things would go wrong ("Why, why, why won't the projector work when I want it to?"), and we'll touch on that in a later chapter, but other things—amazing things—also happened. Sometimes in the training sessions (which at times I did on my own, and other times with my amazing colleagues), there would be participants having "aha" moments, or being so engaged in an activity that they didn't want to stop, and that was food for the soul! The feeling you get when someone walks up to you at the end of the session—"I am so glad I came! You inspired me today! I can't wait to try this with my students!"—is what keeps you hooked, and you don't want to stop doing what you do!

Why did I just spend all this time talking to you about my journey from childhood to adulthood? No, I am not going to give away my age! As a trainer, you have a chance to impact others in a way that very few can. You have an opportunity to teach, to inspire, to create, to collaborate, to network, to learn, and the list goes on! This book shares learnings from my journey as a trainer; in fact, some of these are secrets that I rarely speak about to others! I hope that this helps you in some way, whether it inspires you to try something new or gives you strength to go beyond your comfort zone, or just gives you some ideas of what you can do in your role as a trainer. I sometimes wish I had had that as I entered my role as a trainer, and I am hoping you truly find value in it. Thank you for being a part of this journey! So, let's get started by looking at some of our superheroes! No, I don't mean those that wear costumes (I sometimes see myself wearing a cape, especially with everything I do as a mom!) and have super powers, although some of these individuals may actually have some! Do you want to know who I am talking about? Read on to the next chapter to find out!

But before you do, you will notice that at the end of each chapter, there is a page or two with blank lines. What are they for? Well, an important part of this journey of growth is reflection. In fact, reflection is truly essential for any kind of journey. Take a moment to jot down your thoughts, questions, memories, or ideas on these pages. For those of you who don't like to write in your books, feel free to go to my website, CrushingItOnStage.com, for a bonus handout that you can download and write in.

Back to the superheroes...no, I am not talking about moms and dads, although they certainly qualify!

"We cannot see our reflection in running water. It is only in still water that we can see." – Zen Proverb

Chapter 1 Reflections…

Chapter 2

Trainers as Superheroes!
Looking Back ...

I have had the pleasure of seeing many trainers in action. As I mentioned earlier, some were phenomenal, and others left something to be desired. Admittedly, some were even a huge disappointment!

Okay, so I talked about trainers as superheroes. Why would I do that? When you look back, and you think about the trainers that stood out to you, what was it that they did? What was it that they said to you? How did they say it? How did they make you feel?

I had this one trainer that stood in the hallway and greeted everyone as they were walking in. What a lovely welcoming! Then, as I entered, I noticed that there were some refreshments and snacks, which is always enjoyable! Let's face it, many of us get excited when someone gives us food; and when they don't, we admittedly get a little irritated! At this particular training session, I grabbed my food and sat down. I remember feeling that it was a great start to the day. To top it off, she started on time! It's so refreshing when you have a trainer that starts right on time, because that means they value me and my time; so I loved it.

The lovefest continued! There she was, standing in front of the audience, looking very professional—she was dressed for success, like a powerhouse—and when she spoke, I could feel the energy that she brought into the room! In fact, she was always smiling! Not the kind of smile that's pasted on the face (for the sake of it), but the genuine kind! She was so passionate about her topic. And during the break, she came up to me and called me by my name, asking me where I was from and how I was enjoying the session. She really made me feel like I was important. That is why I talk about trainers as superheroes, because the really great ones make you feel like you can achieve anything. And that's exactly what happened. I actually felt that I could do whatever she put in front of me. That was just one of her superpowers!

Trainers as Superheroes!

You have probably had trainers that were mediocre, and some that truly stood out, almost as the opposite of the superhero, and kind of like a villain in the movie! I think we've all had our share of those. I remember one speaker that will always stand out to me. I was at a month-long program, and there was this one speaker that was really intimidating. During one of his sessions, while I was sitting there with the rest of my peers, he started asking questions. Okay, I know you are thinking, "Umm, that's not a big deal!" Well, hold on a second; I will get there! He would ask a question and then just look at someone randomly in the audience, and ask them to answer it. There was no raising of the hands or anything. And if he knew your name, then he would just turn to you and ask you a question. It was so scary! I remember that I was so nervous that he would pick me that I would look down and avoid any kind of eye contact. Of course, it didn't really matter, because we had name tags on, so he had no problem calling us by our names. I remember the anxiety that people were feeling. You may be wondering how I knew that. Well, I knew that because, at the end of the session, when everyone walked out, you could feel that the room had been drained of its energy. Shortly after, in the safety of my room, my peers began to vent about how it made them feel to sit in his session.

The speaker was brilliant, for sure. But what good is it if you are brilliant, if you leave people feeling that way? Well, a lot of people expressed their frustration in the evaluations that day. Funny enough, the next day, he was going to continue the training, and the project manager actually went to him and told him that people were uncomfortable because of his style of facilitating. The strange thing was that he was legitimately surprised that people felt that way! I suppose we don't always see ourselves through the eyes of the participants. Well, he adjusted his style for the next session, but there were definitely people not present, probably because of how he made them feel the day before. This is why it is so important for participants to be able to share their feedback anonymously, and then have someone actually read them and follow up as needed.

We looked at 2 examples of trainers that left the participants feeling quite differently at the end of the day (almost polar opposites, actually). Let's take another look at the idea of the superhero. A superhero is someone who has special powers and uses them to do good deeds. You can count on them to help you when you need it.

You go to a training session, because either 1) You have no choice, or 2) You want to go there for a specific reason. Besides reasons like missing out on work, getting free food, and hanging out with your colleagues, hopefully you are excited to learn something! The worst feeling you can have is feeling like it was a total waste of your time, and that you could have been doing other more productive things (cat videos anyone?), or feeling like just about anything else would have been more enjoyable (getting rid of those darn nose hairs, perhaps). Okay, that last one was a bit gross, but seriously, the content aside (only because that is often already selected by the higher powers), the trainer is THE most impactful person in that room. When you walk in that room as a participant, you want to feel like you matter, that your perspective matters, and that your time matters.

A trainer has the ability to change perspectives, open minds, empower individuals, and even transform them! How? When a trainer gives you the tools you need for success, shows you how to use them, and more importantly, explains why you need to do it, it can make a world of difference. I know that when I walk into a training session, I want to know that the trainer is competent on the topic, even if they are just there to facilitate and guide me. I also want to know that they have people skills and a personality that I can connect with.

Look, the reality is that you probably can't be a superhero all the time. There will be days when you stand out, and days when you find it hard to connect with the audience. What I do know, from all the years of experience I have had, is that I am a better trainer today than I was when I first started. Why? Is it just that I have figured out what people want, and mechanically do it every time? No! Let's not kid ourselves; being a trainer is hard work. But if you really care about empowering people, about helping them achieve success, you will do what it takes to improve each time you put yourself out there. You have to observe and make notes every time you see a fantastic speaker. Watch how they interacted with the participants, how they facilitated group discussions, how they handled the difficult audience members, how they were able to read the room and know when to have a stretch break, etc.

When you look at the facilitators you have had in the past, what stood out to you? What did you admire? What was important to you?

Go through the list below, and checkmark the features you potentially look for in trainers. It's not a comprehensive list, but it will help you later when you want to strengthen how you do your training sessions.

Appearance

___ Professional-looking
___ Business casual
___ Laid back
___ Very stylish
___ Other: _____

(Do you ever just stare at them and wonder where they got that outfit?)

Personality

___ Very talkative
___ Good listener
___ Loud
___ Quiet
___ Other: _____

(Sometimes some of them don't even need a microphone! But as long as they don't yell too loud, especially if I didn't get enough sleep the night before.)

Content Understanding

___ Must be an expert
___ Should know enough but doesn't have to be an expert
___ It's okay if they don't know anything on the topic, as long as they can facilitate my learning
___ Other: _____

(It's great that some of them are experts, but can they check their egos at the door? Boy, is it irritating when they think they know everything, and that you are so lucky to have them there!)

Style of Facilitation

___ Stand at the front and lecture
___ Walk around and speak
___ Stand on the side and have participants do more of the talking
___ Other: _____

(Not a big fan of the lecture. Kind of reminds me of my childhood!)

Activities

___ There shouldn't be any
___ A minimal amount of engagement
___ Lots of interactive activities
___ Other: _____

(I sometimes dread having to get up and move around. What? Another activity? I just wanted to sleep…)

Ability to read the room

___ Keeps going even though people look bored
___ Is able to pick up on the energy and adjust
___ Reminds audience of the agenda, and tries to get a bit more done
___ Other: _____

(I know a stretch break will help energize me, but so will that donut on the refreshment table...)

People skills

___ Learns my name and uses it
___ Maintains eye contact
___ Doesn't really have any
___ Other: _____

(Boy, does it irritate me when they continue to say my name wrong!)

What was the point of all of that? It's important to take the time to reflect on what you have admired in other trainers. You may have noticed my running commentary after each question. Why did I do that, other than to get a laugh out of you? (There's that goofy side again.) The truth is that we are not always going to be able to please people. In fact, when you were a participant at a session, did you ever feel irritated and wish you were anywhere else? Was it because the trainer was that bad, or you just weren't in the mood to learn? More than likely, you had at least one day like that. I think we have all had those days. This is when you have to pause and acknowledge that you won't always be a superstar (or superhero), that there may be people who won't like those interactive activities you planned, that they aren't in the mood to write in their reflection journal, and that they would just rather check their social media account. IT'S NOT YOU! Well, assuming you do everything you need to do on your part, it probably isn't you!

As I mentioned, it is important for you to make note of the important aspects or characteristics you admire in great trainers. Start a running list. (Use the paper at the end of the chapter to start that.) For those of you who don't like to write in your books, feel free to go to my website, CrushingItOnStage.com, for a bonus handout that you can download and write in.

Does the idea of a trainer as a superhero make you a bit nervous? Are you feeling like, why bother? Don't worry, you don't have to be perfect. No one is. But we all have superpowers. We just have to figure out what they are. Really! The next chapter will help you figure out what yours is!

Trainers as Superheroes!

"I'm reflective only in the sense that I learn to move forward. I reflect with a purpose." – Kobe Bryant

Chapter 2 Reflections…

Chapter 3

I Could Never Do That!

Some of you may be really comfortable on the stage, in front of the audience. Woo hoo! That's great to hear! But some of you may be very scared of being in front of an audience, and that is good. Just to clarify, it's not that it's a good thing, but what I mean to say is that it's good you recognize it. Once you know what the issue is, you can try to come up with a solution that works for you. Note that I said, *"works for you!"* Each one of us is different, and that means you will need to figure out what will work specifically for the challenge you face.

It's important to figure out why you may be scared. I'm not a qualified therapist, but hey, we can still try to think of some potential reasons together. Having a journal to write down some of your thoughts around this would be really helpful. You may use the last page of this chapter, or go to my website, CrushingItOnStage.com, for a bonus handout that you can download and write in.

Here are some potential questions to get you started:

- Was there a time in your past where you had to speak in front of others, and something went wrong?
- What happens to you when you think of going on the stage? (This could be physiological or emotional.)
- Have you ever tried to deal with it in any way (e.g., relaxation or breathing techniques)?
- How severe does it get?

Depending on the severity, getting some help from a physician is probably a great idea. For those that aren't as severe, it may help to try one or more of the following, prior to going up in front of others:

- Start small. (Don't commit to doing a big presentation right away.)
- Try to join a club where you can become a stronger public speaker. (There are many; just do a search on the internet.)
- Ensure you are prepared and know what you are trying

to achieve.
- Talk through what you are going to do, with a colleague or partner.
- Prior to speaking, try a strategy like breathing deeply, 7–10 times, until you start to feel a bit calmer.
- Dress for success (but don't wear something uncomfortable).
- Find a colleague to partner up with—doing it with someone can sometimes be a lot less scary.
- Realize that many people get stage fright, and you are not alone.

We have all been there. I remember one time when I went up in front of an audience to recite a devotional hymn, and a woman sitting in the front row threw me off as she was reciting the same one but with a completely different tune. I tried to stay on track, but honestly, I got so flustered that at the end of my recitation, I pretty much ran out of there. Truthfully, it did take me a bit of time to get back up on a stage again, but I did it; and yes, I had a few more embarrassing moments, even after that. Huh, and you picked up this book thinking I had all the answers! I guess these moments were just a part of my journey that I had to go through. We all have them, and honestly, they may still happen from time to time; but like I said, it is all part of the journey!

Let's take a moment to talk about what your superpowers are—and don't be shy! We all have strengths! If you aren't sure, don't be afraid to go up to a few friends or colleagues and ask them what they think your strengths are. However, make sure you take some time to reflect on it prior to asking them, to see if they see the same things you do.

Here are some examples of potential superpowers you may have, and how they can be beneficial to you as a trainer.

1. Superpower: Organized

You are great at tracking things, handing things in on time, knowing what you have to do and by when, knowing where everything goes, etc.

Benefits for a Trainer:

I bet you can also multi-task! I wish I could! This skill can be beneficial: the planning of the training date; figuring out who will do what; what the agenda will look like; what materials will be needed, and where they will be placed; etc. There is a lot to do when planning a training session! Being organized really makes a huge difference.

2. Superpower: Tech Savvy

You create beautiful presentations and are always ready to try out new technology.

Benefits for a Trainer:

Boy, this is one that many people wish they had! Being tech savvy can be really helpful as a trainer, as you can embed technology to do all kinds of fun and engaging activities, as well as create great visual presentations. It's also extremely helpful when you have technical difficulties during your session!

3. Superpower: Friendly

You love talking to people, and you make friends very easily.

Benefits for a Trainer:

This is a no-brainer! This can be really helpful, as you can start making those one-on-one connections with people, and make them feel comfortable right away.

4. Superpower: Great Sense of Humour

You like to make jokes and are always making people laugh.

Benefits for a Trainer:

This is another no brainer! People like funny people! At this point, I could make a crack about that being the reason you like me, but I guess I may be pushing it. Seriously though, as long as the humour is within limits, it can really help to lighten the mood of training sessions. Just remember the story I shared at the beginning, about not laughing at someone else's expense—a lesson I learned the hard way. If you have a great sense of humour, it can really help everyone to relax and feel more comfortable. A word of caution: When the trainer cracks a lot of jokes, participants may think it is okay for them to do the same, and this can sometimes get out of control. The key is to set the tone of professionalism right from the onset (i.e. humour is clean, appropriate, and in moderation). Having said that, not all kinds of humour will work. For example, dry humour can be difficult for some to understand. The last thing you want is to get no reaction to your jokes. When in doubt, practice it on someone who is typical of your audience (not your best friend or your mom; the two most likely people to laugh at your jokes).

These are just a few of the potential superpowers that can be very helpful for trainers to have. To be honest, we could probably find a benefit for just about any skill. (Okay, maybe not dodging potholes! Why in the world would anyone put that on their resume? True story! Although, if I really thought about it, perhaps this could be helpful for dodging catastrophes in the sessions?) Yes, that was a bit of a stretch, but you get the point. We all have strengths. Figure out what yours are, and then build on that.

I Could Never Do That!

I guess the next area of focus should be on what your weaknesses are. Well, I'm not exactly going there. Let's look at your track record as a trainer. If you are brand new to this, that is fine; you can focus on any opportunities you had in the past, where you spoke in front of a group. (And don't tell me *none*, because we ALL had opportunities when we were younger. Some, we may want to erase, but they did happen!)

When you did your last few training sessions (feel free to reflect on times before that too), take a moment to think about the areas of focus listed below. There may be other areas you would also like to focus on. For each of these, think of what your successes were and what areas you need to grow in (notice I didn't call it a weakness).

- Organization of event (logistics only)
- Facilitation
- Instructional methods and activities
- Participant interaction (yours with the audience, as well as amongst the group)
- Evaluation (during and post event)
- Objectives and outcomes of session
- Impact of training (this is referring to post training – you may or may not have access to this)

Once you have your list, look for patterns, but first focus on the things that went well. What do you see? Is there an area where you excel? Does it correlate to your skills? Is there something you see yourself becoming even better at? This would be a great time to acknowledge and celebrate the amazing things you have accomplished! Great job!

Now for the tough part. (You did know this was coming, right?) What were the areas that you still need to grow in? Do you see patterns here? What would you say are your top 1–2 areas that are non-negotiables, and that you have to work on? So, what do I mean by a non-negotiable? Well, if you found that the participants complained about the food (logistics) a lot, would this qualify as one of the top 2 areas? Probably not. Yes, it's true that food is something that every participant will focus on. Why? Because we love to eat! The problem can be that we all like different things! Some people want healthy food, and some want comfort foods; some like fruit, and some want chocolate desserts. It's like you can't win with them. How do I know? I am one of them! I know fruit is better for me, but I still crave the chocolate desserts! This, however, is an easy fix, so don't put that as your top 2 areas, if it's about food!

If you found that participants complained that they found it boring because all they did was sit there listening to you, then that is a great one to focus on. Don't worry; that also is an easy fix! We'll get to it in one of the later chapters! For now, let's find the major areas you want to focus on. So, why did I say to only look for 1–2 areas? That doesn't mean you just disregard the others, but it often helps if you focus on 1 or 2 things at a time. Improve on those, and then focus on the others. Some may be easy fixes, and that can definitely be done (even if they aren't in the top 2), but for now, focus on the ones that are non-negotiables (i.e. essentials, of which there is no doubt).

So, how are you feeling? Are you still wondering if you can do this? Sometimes half the battle is in our minds. Okay, so you can approach this two ways:

1. Start with the items that are the top 2 areas you need to work on, or
2. Start with the easy wins

Either way is fine. You have to do what works for you. Having said that, if you choose option #2, may I suggest that you don't do that for a major training event you are doing. Perhaps build your confidence by making changes in smaller group sessions. Then, when you are ready, focus on the top 2 things you need to work on.

When working with presenters, I am able to tailor the support to their needs, as we have an opportunity to discuss their top 2 areas that they need to work on. Since you are reading this book (as opposed to sitting opposite me at a coffee shop, eating a delicious chocolate donut), I'm hoping the suggestions within this book will be enough to help you get started on these areas. Feel free to reach out if you need additional support.

There is one thing you can do to help yourself visualize what a successful trainer looks like. Yes, you got it: Go to one of their sessions! Some sessions are even free. Look at some reviews and see what others are saying about them. Although you can even watch a video on the internet that shows them speaking, this will not be sufficient at showing you how they made the audience feel, or what they did before and after the event, or even how they set the event up. Seeing it in person is the best way for you to truly understand. In the meantime, you always have me! I will share my tips with you, but again, I strongly encourage you to find a mentor and observe them. Go up to them and pick their brains. (Okay, maybe not during the session, but set up a time to chat.)

I am a visual learner. I truly learn best when I see things. This is why I am sharing my stories with you. I am hoping you feel like you were present at that time. In fact, I can almost visualize you laughing when you see that woman in the front row, throwing me off with her tune that didn't match mine, but that's okay. I guess it was a bit funny, now that I think about it!

When you feel you are comfortable to try out some of the strategies you have picked up, set up an opportunity for you to try it out at a training session. If you need to have additional support, do it with a colleague; but ensure that you talk through the various elements you want to focus on, prior to doing the session. It's so important that you

I Could Never Do That!

are both on the same page.

Depending on where you are at in your journey, you may want to jump right in, but hold off for now; we haven't gotten into the juicy parts yet! Yes, there's more to come! Next, we will look at what you need to do, now that you are booked to do a training session. Nervous yet? Nah, don't sweat it; it's probably just gas! Now you know why my family groans at my jokes....

"Reflect upon your present blessings—of which every man has many—not on your past misfortunes, of which all men have some." – Charles Dickens

Chapter 3 Reflections…

Chapter 4

Oh No, I've Got to Do the Next Training!

Imagine you just heard from the boss that you need to facilitate the next training session. Woo hoo! It's your time to shine! You can do this! Really! What? That didn't do it for you? Don't worry; by the end of this book, I will have shared a lot of my secrets, so you will be good to go!

But in the meantime, I wanted to share a story that I once heard. A man was walking by some elephants, all of which had chains tied to one of their legs. The man was a bit puzzled, and he went up to the trainer and asked why these elephants weren't breaking free of their chains. You see, the chains were quite thin, and these were powerful elephants. The trainer responded that when the elephants were young, they did try to, but the chains were strong enough to prevent them from breaking away. Although they are the same chains, the elephants have been conditioned to believe they can't break them. Why am I sharing this? Well, besides the horrifying image of these poor elephants being held like that, I think the message is powerful. We may have had experiences in our past that hold us back today from breaking free. If you had one or even a few experiences in front of an audience that didn't go well, this doesn't mean that you can't try again. With time comes experience, knowledge, and a better understanding of what went well and what you could do differently, Embrace it! Embrace the opportunities that lie ahead! But to ensure you have a better experience, let me share more of my tips that have helped me over the years! Now that we are plunging forward, let's focus on what you need to do! When you are given an opportunity to do a training, you need to know what the purpose is. What is it that the participants will walk away with (i.e. the outcomes)? This is critical, as it will impact the planning of your training. First things first. Ask the question: Do you even need a training for this? How many times have you participated in a training session and wondered why it was necessary? I know I have! Ask yourself what they are actually learning. Basically, this is a *needs assessment*, looking at whether there is a deficiency (something needs to be fixed) or an opportunity (something new), and whether training is the best option.

Oh No, I've Got to Do the Next Training!

The three main reasons for training are:

1. To acquire or improve knowledge – An example of this is when there is a new curriculum that the participants will be using to teach the students, but they themselves don't know what it is that they will be teaching! So, yes, in this case, they definitely need the training!

2. To improve or develop a skill – For example, learning an instrument. I've always wanted to learn to play the ukulele (not really, but hey, did I at least get the spelling right? Are you really looking it up? Don't worry; it's right—that's why you pay the big bucks for editors!). Seriously though, a simple example of this is when the participants need to know how to deal with conflict resolution as part of their job—something many of us could benefit from!

3. To improve or gain an attitude/value – There's a new batch of volunteers coming on board, and the staff are not happy about working with them. This may be a good time to deal with this through team building!

Figure out which one of these your training falls under. Is there another way to do it? For example, could a simple communication be enough?

Next, figure out what format would be best suited for this. Examples could include:

- **In-person training** (This can provide an opportunity for more meaningful engagement since participants are there in person.)

- **Self-study modules** (Individuals can do the learning at their own pace, allowing for more flexibility.)

- **Virtual training** (This can be great when you have participants who are in different locations and can't travel.)

- **E-learning modules** (This is good for those that want to do it at their own pace and are tech savvy.)

You may find that this book provides a lot of information for in-person training; however, many of these aspects can also be incorporated into other formats as well. We will go over some of these other formats in more detail, in a later chapter.

Once you know what it is you are training on, the outcomes you need to achieve, and the best suited format, you are on your way! The next important consideration is who the audience is. What do you know about them? For example, do you know the age range, the years of experience, whether they have had any training done on this topic before, how much they know about the topic, what their concerns are, what they hope to get out of the training, etc. If you know the answers to these questions, it really helps you to plan your training more meaningfully. The last thing you want to do is to plan for a virtual session where they will be collaborating online, when most of the participants have never done it before! A lot of time will be spent trying to figure out how to use the platform effectively, and if this extra time was not built in, then it will impact how much you get done.

One way you can find out the information you need is by asking the person who requested the training (in case they have this information already), or by sending out a simple questionnaire to the participants (but ensure it is anonymous so you can get more honest feedback). Frame your questions so you receive the information you need for your training. For example, you may want to ask what work situations they find the most stressful or the most challenging, or what kinds of problems they experience when they are working a specific task. By the way, try to avoid asking the specific age of participants in the questionnaire; sometimes people can be a bit prickly about that kind of thing—perhaps try a range instead! Ideally, doing this online makes it easier for you to access their responses, but a hard copy can also be circulated.

Once you have this information, you can start planning your session! Now, I know it seems like there sure are a lot of steps involved, and you may be feeling overwhelmed, but don't panic yet! Some of this information may be already done for you, and you can just ask for it. I just mentioned it here, so you know that these are the kinds of considerations that help to ensure that your training has the most impact. There may be times when you can skip some of these steps, but take the time to think through it first.

So far, you know the following:

- The purpose of the training (what they are learning/improving)
- The format (how you will do it)
- The background on the participants (who they are, why they need this training, what they are hoping to get out of it)

You probably want to start creating the content for the training, but before you can do that, there is still something you need to do. In some cases, you may already be given the content, or have done this before. (It depends on whether you are a SME—I know, sounds funny, right? A SME is a subject matter expert.) If you don't have it ready, you need to spend some time gathering all the resources you can about the topic. Find out what has been done before. Can you use it as your foundation? Ask about the effectiveness of it; after all, there is a reason they are asking you to do this training. Perhaps the previous training wasn't as effective, or these are new participants who haven't done it yet. The reason I suggest you use it as your foundation, rather than doing it as is, is that there may be other factors to consider (e.g., when it was originally created, it was for a different audience). Content needs to be up to date, relevant, applicable to the real world, appropriate for the participants (i.e. at their level), and meet the purpose and objectives of the session.

If you are a SME, you probably already have the material for your session but may need to adapt it. If you are not, you may need to gather the resources. Something you may want to consider is observing the participants to get a firsthand perspective of what is needed. Talk to the participants (especially if you didn't do a needs analysis or didn't get full participation in it). By asking them firsthand, they will appreciate that you care about their perspective. (Just don't go around looking like a stalker; that will just freak them out.)

While you are gathering your resources, have someone start working on the logistics of the event (unless you have been told to do it all—see, someone sees you as a superhero!). Having a team to work with really helps. Tasks can then be shared amongst team members so that it doesn't become overwhelming for one person. Here are some things you need to consider:

- When to hold the training (date, time), and for how long (e.g., 1 day, a weekend, etc.)
- Where to hold it (unless it is an online event, which will still require some work)
- How to market the training
- How to register participants
- If any work has to be done on their part prior to the training (like reading an article, completing a survey, watching a video)
- What resources you will need
- Budget allocation (someone has to pay for all those sweet treats you plan on providing)

Let's break them down, one at a time. When deciding the date, time, and length of the training, it's a good idea to ensure that there is nothing else going on at that time (like other events). Also, people tend to forget that there is a training the day after the weekend, so you may want to choose a day other than Monday. (Plus, you really don't want to deal with the individuals that are still hungover from partying all weekend.) It can be helpful to know how much time you will need to do the training (which is hard to predict if you haven't developed the content yet, so this may have to be done post planning). If, however, this is something you do on a regular basis, then you probably already know how long it will take to do it. This is important because no one likes to come to a workshop where they were told they had to attend, and then find that the 3-day training could really have been done in 1 day.

This will be something you will need to remember as you are planning (i.e. no fluff; everything must have a purpose).

One question you may have is, where should you hold your training if it is an in-person session? You could hold it in the workplace (so no one needs to travel further), but this doesn't always work; one reason being the space restrictions. Another reason why this may not work is if you want to create an ambiance that the space does not allow for. For example, if you want to have the participants feel like they are getting away (this can help create a more energized space for the learning), you may want to look outside for another venue. The best places for that would be hotel banquet halls, but this can be really pricey, so budget will play a big role in the decision making. Keep in mind the travel distance to the venue, access to parking, and proximity to the bus and subway. You want to make it as easy as possible for the participants to be able to get to the event. The last thing you want is for them to find other reasons why they can't attend.

Wherever you choose to hold it, these are some of the factors you should consider:

- Overall set-up of space
    * Where will the participants sit?
    * Will tables be needed?
    * Where will the trainer or facilitator be?

* Where will refreshments be served?
* Where will the AV be set up?
* Where will the registration table go?
* Is there space on the walls to post up charts from the session?

- Set-up of chairs/tables (This will be dependent on several factors, like the content of training and the number of participants.)
   * U-shape, half rounds, circle of chairs, classroom style, boardroom, etc.

- Lighting (Natural light, or lighting that simulates daylight, decreases stress and increases learning, but having shades is important, especially if using a projector for which a dark room is necessary.)

- Room temperature (Between 20 and 22 degrees Celsius is generally a good temperature; you don't want it too warm, where people are falling asleep, or so cold that people can't even think.)

For other formats, like self-study modules, and virtual and e-Learning, you will need to ensure that either you or someone in the IT department can support your technical needs. The budget for these formats will be a lot less, but the format may not be the best for your purpose, so that decision will need to be made earlier.

Oh No, I've Got to Do the Next Training!

Marketing the training is key because, let's face it, if you don't let people know what you are doing and when, you may be sitting all alone (except for your best friend who came to support you). My colleagues and I have definitely faced that challenge before, but thankfully, it was a webinar format, so the budget was minimal. We figured even 1 person trained is better than none, but this doesn't make up for the time spent in preparation, or our time to do the session—not to mention that poor soul who did join and had to do it all by themselves. (That meant they had to pay attention in case we asked questions!) It was a good thing we recorded it, so it could be used for training others. My point? Like I said, marketing is key! Start it early, and consider different formats (do you need to use social media?), and send reminders. I like to include the registration link in the marketing, so I know who is thinking about coming. Having said that, one thing I quickly realized is just because someone signed up, doesn't mean they will come!

Ensure your marketing is visually appealing, gives details (like day, time, and place) and a brief overview of what the training will cover, in addition to the registration link. If participants have to pay (in case it is a public event), provide a way to do that. Sometimes you can ask them to pay a certain amount to hold their spot, and share that they will be reimbursed when they attend, but this may be a turnoff to some. Having participants register allows you to know who is thinking of coming, and also gives you access to their information (e.g., email address), and if you wanted to ask questions in advance (like I suggested earlier), this can be a good time to do it. If you want participants to do something prior to attending the session (other than the questionnaire), you can send a follow-up email (once you have their email addresses) in advance. However, just be cautious of asking them to do something that will take a lot of time, or sending it last minute, as it could prove to be a major deterrent for them showing up.

Your resource list will be heavily dependent on the content of the training (which we will get to in the next chapter); however, certain things you may already know, such as a sound system and microphone, tables and chairs (again dependent on your numbers), table for food (hmmm, do I mention that a lot?), and tables for registration, supplies, etc., plus other AV equipment (projector, screen, etc.), as well as a music playlist. (This will be discussed further, in Chapter 6.) Having resources, like mini white boards (even plastic plates from the local dollar store) and dry erase markers, can be a great way to get everyone participating at the same time (instead of just a few people responding to questions). You will need to revisit your list, and add as needed, once you have storyboarded your session and know which activities you will be doing.

And lastly, but probably the most important, is the budget. You may not have much of one, which will have big implications on the kind of training you do (e.g., webinar vs in-person) and the venue of it (if in-person), so I strongly recommend you find out right away what it is, and then start planning. If this is a yearly event, ensure that it is already submitted in advance for the following year (especially if you want to increase the budget and try new things). It there are options for getting some of the resources for cheaper or for free, try to arrange for that by looking for sponsors or donations. Sometimes the topic can allow for that. You may also need additional manpower, which will add on to the cost, unless you can find some volunteers to help out, but ensure that they are reliable and willing to follow your standards (e.g., how to communicate with the participants—the last thing you want is for the volunteers to be rude and roll their eyes when the participants are making certain requests).

Hopefully, this chapter gave you a lot of food for thought. I know the content was a lot more technical. Why? Well, besides the fact that I can't just share stories of the mishaps in my life, by the end of the book, I want you to feel confident that this is something you can do. If you are already doing a lot of these things, that's wonderful! That means you are on the right track! So, what's next? Now that you have the basics covered, it's time to start putting the content together and figuring out exactly what you will be doing. This is the fun part! You get to decide whether people will walk away thinking the training was either dull or dynamic. Tune in to the next chapter to ensure that your sessions are *dynomite!*

"Efforts and courage are not enough without purpose and direction." – John F. Kennedy

Chapter 4 Reflections...

Chapter 5

I'm Ready to Start. Now What?

You want to have the kind of training sessions that excite, energize, and empower. How do you go about doing that? You need to plan, plan, and plan. Did I mention that planning is the key? If you are doing the training with another individual, or a group of individuals, it's critical that the planning is done as a joint effort, to ensure you don't have issues last minute about why things weren't done a certain way. It really helps to have a team to work on the details together, as it can sometimes seem overwhelming if you do everything yourself (and it helps to have someone to bounce ideas off).

So far, we have discussed the importance of the following:

- The purpose of the training (what they are learning/improving)
- The format (how you will do it)
- The background on the participants (who they are, why they need this training, what they are hoping to get out of it)
- Gathering all the resources for the content
- The logistics (including the budget)

Although we spoke about finding out who the participants are, one thing that is important is to think about how these participants will learn best. If you are training children, you will do things quite differently than if you are working with adults. The last thing you want to be doing is treating adults like children, although sometimes this can be okay. What? I know you think that I'm not making much sense, but give me a moment to explain. If, for example, you are training teachers, you can model how they would use a certain strategy in the classrooms. In this case, it is okay to treat them like children. Having said that, you may want to say that from the get-go. I have personally seen adults who were offended when they were spoken to like kids. When I am working with teachers, I always state at the beginning of the session, how I will be modeling what I would say and do, as if I was in the classroom. This way, they understand why you are doing it. Having said that, on occasion I do get the pleasure of having a participant who does a great job of acting like a student in the classroom (you know, the smart aleck who likes to heckle during the session). I often joke about how teachers make the worst students (especially when you ask a question, and no one raises their hands!).

When working with adults, it's important to think about the principles of adult learning (refer to Malcolm Knowles for more information). These include the following:

- They want to know what they are learning and why (having their buy-in makes it so much easier).
- They want to be involved in the process (e.g., being asked what kind of training they feel they could use, to do their job more effectively).
- They come with a wealth of experiences and knowledge. (When we tap into these experiences, we validate them.)
- The relevance of the training must be apparent and be focused on something that is addressing a problem. (They need to know that what they are learning will impact them now.)
- They are internally motivated to learn (and will come back for more if they feel there is value in what is being done).

Knowing all of that, we are ready to proceed to the storyboarding of the session. This is when you figure out the sequence of the content to be taught, as well as how to do it. One great way to do this is with the use of Post-it notes. On the Post-it notes, put down a concept or learning you want to focus on—one thought per note. Once that is determined, you can choose a different colour Post-it for instructional methodologies you want to use. This can help you visualize what the training will look like, and ensure you have considered all types of learners (e.g., visual, kinesthetic, and auditory). After you have adjusted them to ensure you have a balance of activities with teaching moments, you can start to plan the different aspects of it, and include transitions in between the different activities to help ensure that each one builds on the other. Ensure you put in suggested timings for each section, and adjust as needed. I can't emphasize how important it is to build in buffer time for activities that take much longer due to numbers, or because of the questions that the participants have. Another important element to build in to the day is an opportunity for participants to share their experiences and best practices. As you are creating the outline of what the day will look like, embrace your strengths and uniqueness, and embed aspects of that within the day. That's one way of making yourself stand out as a trainer. For example, I am known for my crazy and goofy side. I usually show that through my training by embedding humour throughout the day.

I'm Ready to Start. Now What?

There are basic things that need to be included in your storyboard:

- Intro (welcome, housekeeping, speaker bio, expectations – optional)
- Inspiring start (hook, reviewing agenda and outcomes)
- Team builder/icebreaker activities
- Activities (content to be covered, instructional strategy, and assessment strategy)
- Brain-break activities
- Closing (inspirational ending, evaluation)

Although you may not need all of these, it helps to have extra ideas ready in case you need them (especially brain breaks—no, that is not *code* for nap time—see explanation below).

Prior to starting the session, it's helpful to go over housekeeping matters right away (for example, where the washrooms are, what the plan is for the day, what time breaks are—which is what most of them want to know right away—as well as other things that may come up). This can be done easily by creating a slide and having it displayed on the screen as the participants enter, or can be shared by whoever is starting the day off.

During the welcoming, you may choose to have someone introduce you by going over a short bio, showcasing some of your achievements, in case they are not familiar with you. This should be short and sweet. It helps validate why you are the right person to do the training, but it should not be a brag session (no one likes one of those)!

Depending on the kind of session it is, I sometimes take time on the first day to have participants brainstorm the kind of environment that is conducive to learning for them. Although I facilitate this (as opposed to telling them), I find that when they come up with this, there is more buy-in (ahh, now you see how the adult principles factor in). Ideally, this is written on chart paper (having an audience member as a scribe really helps) and then posted on the wall where they can all see. It's important that everyone buys into this. If it is a large group, I sometimes break them into smaller groups to do this. We then post the charts up and look for commonalities, and that then becomes our group norms. So, why am I bringing it up here? Prior to the day, I draft up my own expectations that are important (for example, phones put on vibrate or sound muted, people stepping out to take calls, coming to the sessions prepared to learn), and then, on the day of the training, I guide the conversation to the topic if it hasn't already been mentioned. Yes, I know this comes off as being very sly, but I like to think of it as being clever! Most of the time, these are also important to the participants, but they just didn't think of it at the time.

Once those details are out of the way (and hopefully, it didn't take you long to do), you want to start off with a

I'm Ready to Start. Now What?

hook, something that grabs their attention. Hooks can include a short video, a story, a powerful quote, or an image, just to name a few. The hook sets the tone for the session. If you grab their interest right from the get-go, this can go a long way in ensuring they are open to the kind of learning taking place in the training. Whatever you choose, ensure it is relevant and somehow connects to the purpose of the training. I am a big proponent of storytelling (whether it is a personal one or a story created by someone else), especially when the speaker has a dramatic flair for doing this. Think back to your favourite speaker. How did they start off the session? I remember hearing one speaker talk about her personal journey and how she dealt with her cancer. It was truly inspirational how she used her journey to help others along the way, and this was her segue into how important it was to do voluntary service. Now, I'm not saying that you go and find a health concern as part of your hook (and no, ongoing constipation issues don't count), but find something that can truly get your point across.

Perhaps there is an image or video that stands out to you. I remember using one particular video in a session I did. The video showed how a village was at a standstill due to a storm, and no one wanted to do anything about a tree that had fallen in the middle of the road. You could see the long line of traffic all because of the tree. Suddenly, a young child started to walk by everyone as he headed toward the tree. At that point, raindrops started to fall, but he kept walking toward the tree. When he got there, he dropped his school bag and stood there pushing as hard as he could to move the tree. Others around him stopped what they were doing and just watched him; and some even laughed at the scene of this little kid trying to move such a large tree. A moment later, other children started running up to where he was, and began to help him push the tree. You could see them laughing in the rain as they tried to pick up the tree. The whole scene was quite ridiculous but moving at the same time! One by one, you could then see adults moving toward the children, and they too started to help. Shortly after, with the help of the whole group (adults and kids), they were able to pick up the tree and move it to the side of the road; so now everyone could get through. This powerful video was just two and a half minutes long. After playing it for the participants, I asked them what message they got out of it, to which there were varied responses. After acknowledging their thoughts, I connected it to what we were working on that day by focusing on the potential impact one individual can have (and how easy it is to underestimate an individual based on factors like age). It was great to see how impactful a short video clip could be. It got the attention of the group, and we were then well on our way to a great start to the day.

Another really important element of the start to the day is going over what it is that they are going to learn (sharing of the objectives and outcomes). If a survey was done prior to the training, I would share how their input helped me to create the content of the session. This validates the participants and, hopefully, sets the tone that the training will be working toward their needs. I like to go over the agenda as well. I sometimes come up with creative or funny headings for the agenda items, just to keep them wondering what we will be doing. For example, if I was going to do an activity around the fear of public speaking, I would put a heading like "Fear Factor" on the agenda. It may sound silly, but I find that these little things make it fun and interesting for the participants (and no, I didn't make participants eat weird food or insects in that activity, like the television show with that name).

It can sometimes help to start off with an icebreaker or team building activity. I like to have it connected somehow to the topic, as I believe that no opportunity should be wasted. Participants are here for a reason, and I don't like to waste their time with frivolous activities. The only time I wouldn't do this is when I feel that the participants need a bit more time to feel comfortable prior to doing activities like this. An example of a team building activity could be for the team to come up with a tower made from paper and tape. All teams receive 3 sheets of paper, scissors, and a certain amount of tape. The team with the tallest structure (not leaning against anything) is the winner. In the end, I would probe the teams to come up with their learnings, such as the importance of working as a team (listening to each other's ideas, collaborating, each member having a role, etc.), and what happens when there is a break down. Sometimes icebreakers are about getting to know other participants, so the activity would be around that; but again, the questions would be selected in advance, keeping in mind the topic being focused on in the session.

I would then go into the content (building on what has been discussed already). The content can be presented in different ways. If I am creating a slideshow presentation, I ensure that the slides have minimal text, with visuals that help the participants understand the message (and not distract) and, if needed, I provide handouts. When I put together the slides, I draft up speaking notes to go along with them, and I try to keep them minimal. Believe me when I say no one likes to have the slide read back to them! I always check back to ensure that the content on the slides covers points that are working toward the outcomes that I want the participants to walk away with. I'm also big on formatting. Anything that I show or hand out must look professional. I don't like spelling or grammatical errors. It helps to have a fresh eye look at the material just in case you miss something. There are so many great templates and presentation tools available that it is worth the effort to try something new. Images should be selected carefully (there are lots of sites where you can get access to free images), and videos and audio can be integrated straight into the presentation. If charts or visuals are displayed, ensure there is colour and that they are large enough for the participants to see. There is no point in having it if they can't see it!

As I have already mentioned, think about who your audience is and what kinds of activities would be appropriate. Having said that, there are so many activities you can do (although you may get an initial groan from the audience) that they will have a blast by the end of it. Just make sure that it connects to what you are doing. Another way you can be mindful of your audience is when you are picking resources and metaphors. Be aware of the diversity that exists, as you don't want to offend any of your participants. This applies even to something as simple as your handouts. You may want to reduce the font size so you can get it all on 2 pages, but for someone who is visually impaired, this can be very frustrating. One way to do this is by asking participants (in the registration) if they have special requests that will help you create a more meaningful experience for them. This is a learning I had when I had a participant raise this concern in one of my trainings.

I like to ensure participants are interacting with the content. Although some like to take notes on their computer, I often encourage participants to take written notes where possible, as there is a greater retention rate when you actually write it with your hand. Handouts that have *fill in the blanks* are a great way to ensure participants are listening intently, and it saves them time from writing everything down. They only have to fill in the missing sections, but I also provide space in case they want to write more.

It helps to have brain breaks approximately every 45 minutes, so I plan them ahead of time and have a bank of them ready in case I need them. Brain breaks are 2–3 minute activities that provide participants with a burst of energy, ideally helping them to refocus on the task or learning. This is especially needed right after lunch. How many times have you been at a session and started to fall asleep because you chose to eat pasta instead of going for the light chicken and salad option? (You may as well get a pillow and find a corner for a nap! Just try not to drool or snore too loudly.)

After providing the participants with new learning, it is so important that they have an opportunity to engage with it. Ideally, you would want to ensure participants are active every 5–7 minutes. Some researchers even go as far as saying the average attention span is 3 minutes, so you know you need to be observing the audience and keeping them engaged! Some options you could do include having participants reflect on what was said, write in a journal, turn to their elbow partner to discuss something, complete a worksheet, movement to transition to the next activity, etc. If your training involves learning a skill, it's important that enough time is provided for the participants, in addition to access to the equipment (e.g., computers, instruments, etc.). There are many interactive strategies

I'm Ready to Start. Now What?

that can create spaces of engagement in a meaningful manner. Remember, anything that you want them to use when they leave, should be modeled while they are at the training session. Have them think about how this learning applies to their role.

As I just mentioned, whether they are doing activities in groups or in pairs, there are so many interactive activities they can be doing, such as looking at scenarios or case studies, small group discussions, quizzes and polls, guided imagery, working on graphic organizers, etc. Check out my website for an enhanced list of different activities that they can be doing to engage with the learnings. The more active they are in their learning, the greater the retention level. Once you know what you want to do and when (remember, you need for them to be active every 5–7 minutes), create a step-by-step list of how they will do it. Providing written instructions for activities is helpful for those that need to see the instructions themselves.

Think about assessment. How will you ensure that they are actually learning? Being present doesn't mean that the learning took place. Trust me! I can think of many sessions where I don't remember what we even discussed. Call it old age; call it what you will. It is reality. Providing opportunities for the participants to reflect on what they learned, and to apply the new learnings, is important. This can take place in different ways. You will need to decide on whether this can be done in groups or done individually, depending on the purpose and objectives of the training. Are you doing it to get a general idea of whether the participants understand the concepts, or do you want to know what every individual has learned? Take some time to think about the kinds of questions you want to ask. Should they be open ended or closed? Refer to Bloom's Taxonomy to help you determine the kinds of questions you want to ask.

In all cases, ensuring participants feel safe and comfortable to respond is important. Creating an ethos of respect and trust (that others will not laugh at them) is important for all trainers to do. Some fun ways to engage learners and to assess their thoughts and learnings include online polls and quizzes. This can be done individually or in groups. If anonymity is okay, this can be a lot of fun and not cause anxiety. You can also have groups discuss scenarios, act out solutions, and create resources (e.g., job aids that embed the learnings), as well as follow tutorials using the equipment provided. Social media can also be a platform for participants to share their reflections and learnings (#BestSessionEver).

One fun strategy I like to use, just as a quick way to see how participants are feeling, is an exit ticket. Right before lunch, I ask them to fill out a paper, listing 3 things they learned or found value in, 2 questions they have, and 1 thing they would like to have modified for the next session (if possible). This way, I can get a pulse of how the participants are feeling, and I can adjust whatever is possible for the rest of the day. This can be done at the end of the day as well.

You have planned the content and the activities that will help them to engage with it and put it in a document (from the Post-it notes that were created earlier). Now what? Well, you need to go through it until you have internalized it. Go through the slides and say them out loud (the more you practice, the more comfortable you will feel). Visualize yourself there, talk to yourself in the mirror, or record yourself! If possible, even go to the venue and practice. I know it's going to look odd (especially if someone walks by while you are talking to yourself), but it will help. I promise!

As you prepare for the big day, keep in mind that things may not always go as planned. (Believe me, I speak from experience.). One thing that happens quite often is technical difficulties. Maybe your microphone won't work, or the video isn't playing with sound, or the internet isn't connecting. When those things happen (and we all have them happen at one time or another), be prepared to keep going without them. Talk louder, move closer to the participants, use an easel to write, sit in a circle and talk, describe the video, have participants stand up and sit down to respond to true or false questions, etc. There are things you can do to be as proactive as possible; for example, download the videos onto your computer, have a backup microphone, have chart paper ready, have handouts of the slides printed, connect your laptop to your phone and use it as a hotspot, and get there very early and try out everything. Have someone support all your IT needs so you don't have to worry about them. One other tip when trying to be proactive is to foresee any questions or issues that may be raised, and come up with potential ways to respond to them.

Once you know what you are doing and when, come up with a list of all the resources you will need for each section, and start collecting them. It isn't always easy to know how many copies you will need of handouts, which is why having participants register in advance is helpful, but you always need to have extra copies on hand as you may get last minute registrations (and hopefully, your photocopier doesn't break down like mine has before, which is why you need to get them done in advance and not the day before!). One fun thing that can be incorporated on the day of training is having some kind of a draw. Decide in advance if and how you would like to do this. Some trainers like to do it as a way of rewarding those that get there early (an incentive). They get to enter into a raffle or draw by depositing the ticket they received as they entered, into a box. It can sometimes be nice to give everyone an opportunity, so all participants get a ticket, but perhaps those that arrive on time get two! You will need to figure out what you will be giving away at the end of the training session. (For example, perhaps you want to give away a book; or if you have sponsors, you can get some great giveaway prizes.)

Feeling prepared yet? Don't worry; if you have been following along and doing what we discussed, you pretty much have it all under control! It's true that things don't always go the way we plan (for example, the venue you wanted is no longer available), but don't stress over it. Have contingency plans, and make the best of the situation. Next, we will look at what you can do on the day of the training to ensure it is smooth sailing, as well as tips on how to end the day!

"How we think shows through in how we act. Attitudes are mirrors of the mind. They reflect thinking." – David Joseph Schwartz

Chapter 5 Reflections...

I can do this!

Chapter 6

Ahhh! The Big Day Is Here!

I bet, at this point, you are truly wishing you had nerves of steel! Like I said earlier, I honestly get nervous every time I do a session. Personally, I think anyone who doesn't get nervous is either not being honest or is just really passive about the whole thing (probably because they have been doing the same thing for years)—and who wants a speaker that spews things out like a machine? I figure that someone who is nervous will go out of their way to be prepared and do what it takes to be successful. When you become too comfortable, you don't push yourself, and it shows in your lack of passion.

What can you do to ensure things go as smoothly as possible on the day of the training? Like I said in the last chapter, show up early (as early as possible). You don't have control over traffic (unless you live nearby or are staying at the hotel where the session is being held). Remind everyone that is supporting or doing the session with you to be there early as well. If you are on your own, get some help—that's what family is for! Ensure everyone has assigned tasks in advance so things get done quickly.

Ideally, the setup of the room was done in advance (depending on the venue chosen), but it is best to double check that everything is exactly as requested. For a ready-to-use checklist, refer to my website. Check the ventilation, heating, and air conditioning for comfort. Find out where the washrooms and fire exits are. Set up the equipment for your training (laptop, projector, screen, etc.), and ensure that any audio or videos you are showing, work. Make sure you have requested the Wi-Fi password, and check that the internet is connected (if needed). Test the microphone and sound system, and make note of any audio feedback—which is often the screeching sound you hear when the microphone is too close to the speaker (don't you just hate it when that happens?)—and adjust the microphone or speaker as needed. Have a remote for your presentation, and ensure you are mindful of where the projector is, to avoid standing in front of it. The last thing you want to do is to cover up what is on the slide, with your body!

Ahhh! The Big Day Is Here!

Have soft music playing in the background. Decide what works best for you. Personally, I like current music (clean versions, of course) that gets you moving to the beat. This can be played as people are walking in, during breaks, at the end of the day, and sometimes even during group work if it is soft enough (although some prefer soft classical music for this). Ideally, this playlist has been created in advance, so you don't have to worry about it on the day of.

Registration lists and name tags can be placed near the entrance, along with any handouts that need to be given out at the beginning of the day. Note that labels used as name tags often fall off and don't last for more than 1 day. It's best to use name tags that have been printed in advance (large font) and placed in badge holders with a lanyard. Ideally, you want the lanyard to be short enough that you can see the person's name without bending down to read it. Having them printed double-sided is best: just in case they flip over, you can still read the name. I find that most people prefer the lanyard over the badge that has to be pinned on. Who knew name tags could be so complicated! Just remember to have some extras on hand for those that register late (and a thin marker for them to print their name).

It can also be helpful to have extra pens and notepaper for those that may have forgotten to bring theirs. If you are giving some tickets for a draw, have them ready at this station (with someone manning the table). Note that you will need a box for these tickets to be placed in. If you are going to ask participants to complete a printed evaluation form, provide it as they enter so they can write their thoughts as the session progresses.

Follow up to ensure that the refreshments are ready and set up as needed. It's always nice to provide tea, coffee, and water throughout the day, as a minimum. Food items always provide excitement (or is it just me?), and can be a nice way to start the day.

Post up a chart titled as the "Parking Lot," with Post-it notes nearby, where participants can post any questions they have. These can be addressed throughout the day, as applicable. This is especially helpful at the beginning of the training, when participants may not be comfortable asking questions yet. Assign someone to check these periodically throughout the day.

Another chart that is good to post up is the agenda of the day. This helps keep you accountable, and also benefits the participants, as they can then anticipate the next transition. Somewhere in the room, you can also post up the Wi-Fi password and any other pertinent information they will need.

Depending on who the participants are, I often have an additional chart in which I track the strategies that I am modelling. I ask the participants to point them out, and if they miss anything, I add on to the list.

Have someone ready to be your timer. (They can hold up a white board with the amount of time you have left in your session.) If you don't have anyone to do that, print out a copy of your agenda (with actual start and stop timings) to help you gauge how much time you have left. Place all supplies (markers, chart paper, handouts, etc.) on a table that is accessible, in the order of when they will be needed, in order to save time.

Once you are ready (hopefully, in advance of the arrival of the participants), then you should ensure you go to the washroom. (It gets more difficult once the day has started.) If you are a teacher, you probably can hold it for most of the day (not a healthy option for sure, but the reality). I know it sounds strange to include this, but it's so important! I'm not sure what the statistics say about the percentage of trainers and speakers who have bladder infections, but I wouldn't be surprised if it is high! Another important aspect is to ensure you have eaten and are staying hydrated. Keep a reusable water bottle near you, and drink whenever you can.

As participants start to walk in, it's important that you have your name tag, and that you are there to greet them as they enter. Thank them for coming, and if they have their name tag on, use their name when you speak to them.

Keep smiling (not one that is pasted on your face, but one that actually shows how happy you are to be spending the morning/day with them). If you have time, strike up a conversation with them, asking them about where they drove in from, or if they found parking okay. Try to keep it light, and don't ask them questions that they need to really think about (at least not when they just walk in). If you know the participants, ask how the family is doing, or if they have done anything interesting lately. Focus on them. If you can tell that they are uncomfortable sharing personal information, you can share something you did recently; but generally, it's nice when you show you are interested in them.

Make sure you start the day on time, even if you have only a few people there at that time. You can adjust the plan slightly, and perhaps talk about something that is okay if people miss it (like housekeeping, which can always be repeated right before a break, for those that missed it). By doing this, you are showing that you value and respect their time. If you have additional days in the training, it will also set the precedence that participants need to show up on time. Having said that, don't humiliate anyone who comes in late. (You don't know what they went through that morning.) No one likes to be embarrassed in front of others. It's not how you want the participants to remember you. If you are creating the group norms or rules, make sure you do it right away, as it sets the tone for the day.

Ahhh! The Big Day Is Here!

As you talk to the participants, smile and try to relax. Make a joke if something doesn't work, and then try a different approach. Be flexible! Things don't always go as we planned. How we react to it, makes a statement. You want to be modeling professionalism throughout the day. Refer to your notes as needed, but try to make it fluid by looking at the audience when you talk. Ensure you are looking at everyone (and not just at one side of the room). Don't be afraid if you forget something (no one will know but you), and remember that you can always mention it later. I like to walk around among the participants, but the challenge with that is that if you are talking and walking, some people may only be seeing your back. If you aren't using a microphone (this would only happen if the group and room were small in size), then be aware that as you walk, people may not be able to hear you.

One great strategy is to walk toward someone when they are asking you a question. Then, as you move back to where you were, repeat the question (in case others didn't hear it), and then respond. Always be cognizant of others in the room, ensuring they can hear you and others who may be speaking. If you are asking the question, give them some think time, and then take responses. Remember that when you are asking a question, try to engage as many people as possible. One great way of doing this is by using a sentence starter, like "Raise your hand if you...." Another way of doing this is by asking participants to repeat what you said (keep it short!), or by having them give you a thumbs up or thumbs down. You can also point out if there is something they should write down in their notes. Remember, you want to keep them moving every 5–7 minutes! But when it comes to questions...have you ever been present when a facilitator told someone their answer was excellent, and yet just nodded at yours? How did you feel? I recently saw a trainer ask her participants a question but then honour all responses (and as an FYI, at that same session, she played a game; and although the winning team got to choose their prize, she ensured all participants got one too). I loved how she handled the situation, ensuring everyone felt like a winner!

There may be times when you don't know the answer to a question that you are asked, and that is completely okay. After all, as much as I like to believe I know everything (at least that's what I tell my daughters, especially the youngest one!), there are many things I don't. One way to handle a situation like that is to acknowledge the wonderful question that was just shared, and then to throw the question back out to the audience for their thoughts. Another one is to simply say that it was a great question, and that you will reflect on it and get back to them with a response a bit later (which should be honoured). At times, you may even find participants asking a question that is way off tangent. If you feel that the audience would benefit from your response, take the time to speak to it (even if it throws off your agenda somewhat). You can even share that with them prior to giving your thoughts. If you feel that it is a random question that you don't have time for at that moment, thank them for the question (so important to honour them) and then ask if they are okay if you can speak about it further at the end of the session.

When you are ready to do group work or activities, try forming them based on how they are seated. In some cases, you may not have a lot of room for them to spread out, so perhaps they can just turn to the people sitting behind them and form a group. I like to model different ways they can get into groups. This can be fun and really wake up people (in case they were falling asleep), as they often have to walk around to get into their group. This also helps break up the groups that came and sat together because they know each other. It's best to have a few strategies prepared in advance so you don't have to figure it out on the spot. I like to give instructions prior to people moving, to avoid having them ask later, as they were too busy figuring out where they had to go. In fact, one great strategy is to ask someone to repeat what the steps are, prior to starting. Half the time, the trainer isn't clear in the instructions, so the task doesn't get completed the way it was meant to. By having a participant repeat it, you can ensure that it was understood.

Walk around as they are discussing in their groups. Try to get a pulse of what they are saying so you can touch on some of these points when you debrief the activity. At times, you may need to probe them further with a question or two, in case you feel they need the support. The participants often come with a wealth of experiences, and tapping into that is key! Having said that, sometimes they just need a nudge in that direction (note the nudge, and not push!). Make note if you find one or two people who do most of the talking. You want to create safe spaces where everyone has a voice. One way I do that is by suggesting different roles that members can choose from (e.g., the reporter, the recorder, the time manager, the resource manager, etc.); although they all have to contribute, it helps ensure team members are participating. When I do use team roles, I always explain what each of them would do, prior to them doing it. I also encourage people to take on a different role each time, which prevents the same person from sharing when it is time to present in front of the whole group.

It's not easy to be the one presenting (although some individuals love to talk!), and as a trainer, it's important that you support each participant as much as possible (encouragement is key). Having guidelines on the presentations is strongly recommended. For example, each presenter has 2 minutes to share 1–2 points that were discussed. The next group can only share new points. This prevents the whole group from having to hear the same points repeatedly, which can lead to participants losing interest in what is being presented, and opens the door to side conversations that can be very distracting (not to mention unfair) to the person sharing.

Ahhh! The Big Day Is Here!

Getting the attention of the participants, when they are in their groups, can be a challenge in itself! I usually use an attention grabber and wait until everyone is paying attention (which can sometimes take a minute or two). I usually use a call and response strategy, which can be a lot of fun. The facilitator shouts out a word/sentence, like *Hakuna*, and the audience replies with a response to it, which in this case would be *Matata*. Another way of grabbing their attention is by clapping a rhythm with your hands, and having the audience clap the same rhythm back. Another strategy I saw a facilitator use is to say a word or phrase in an unusual manner, and have the audience repeat it the same way—for example, "Hellooooo there!" and they would repeat it back. It's just a fun way of grabbing attention as opposed to saying, "Can I get everyone's attention?" When I am doing a training for teachers, I often remind them to teach the students the strategy prior to using it, so they know what the expectation is. This can be helpful to other participants as well. A word of caution: It is critical to know your audience, and to choose strategies and frame things based on this knowledge. There is this one attention grabber that I had used in many contexts, and it was well received. When I used it during an international training session, I was surprised to hear that one of the words in the phrase had another connotation in their context that wasn't very nice. (Yes, you can imagine how awkward that situation was!) It's another example of how I am still learning!

Back to the training! There are several things you want to end your session with. First, go over the main points of the session, not taking a lengthy amount of time but just a quick summary of what was covered. An effective way of doing this is by asking the participants to share their highlights. Having someone scribe on a chart paper is helpful for those that need to visualize what was said. Add on anything that was missed (either by probing through a question or by showing a visual, or using a sentence starter as a prompt). If you want to make it fun, you can even have an object as a microphone. This gets passed around, and you can only share when you have it in your possession! Admittedly, I remember one of the first times I tried it; I used the only thing I could get my hands on at that time, which was a tennis ball. At the precise moment that the boss of my boss walked in, a participant whipped the ball to another person in the room, and it hit them in the head! My learning? Ensure it is a soft, cushion-like ball that is tossed! Don't worry; no one was seriously hurt, except maybe my ego!

Second, if you ask the participants to do anything, it is critical that you do a follow-up. This would be a good time to go over the parking lot questions (remember the chart you set up at the beginning?) and respond to any that are outstanding.

Third, have them share how they can use these learnings in their roles. (This is the answer to the question: "I learned this, so now what?") It is so important that they walk away with a good understanding of how this knowledge can now help them. (Refer back to the 3 main reasons for training.) One example of a quick activity you can do is for them to share what they will now STOP, START, or CONTINUE, based on what was learned.

Fourth, flash the outcomes that you aimed to cover in the session; and hopefully, they were all met. Ideally, you want to be tracking this yourself throughout the session to ensure all of them are covered. It is important for them to see that you covered everything you said you would do. This adds to your credibility.

Fifth is the conclusion of the session. We talked about the importance of how you start the session (remember the hook?), but the end of the session/day is just as important! You want to end with something powerful, with them thinking, "Wow! That was incredible!" In fact, there is something called the primacy/recency effect. In basic terms, this refers to how people often retain what happened at the beginning and at the end, more than the middle. Therefore, it is critical to start off a session with a bang, and end with a similar effect! When you do that, the participants will walk away remembering these! You can start it by making acknowledgments (to any co-facilitators, support staff, mentors, and most importantly, the participants for their engagement in the session). Then, close it off with some inspiration, such as a powerful quote or story that sums up the topic well.

Lastly, have them complete the evaluation, which hopefully, you handed out at the beginning of the session and reminded them to fill out throughout the day.

Truth be told, training sessions don't always end on time—sometimes because of the amount that is jam packed into the day; sometimes because the participants needed more time on a particular topic. Either way, if you find that you need to extend the day even by 5 minutes, it's important to ask permission from the participants, thereby honouring them.

If you were already nervous, this is truly not meant to make things worse! One thing I have learned over the years is that if you lead with your heart, you will never fail! Sure, there may be times when you wish it had gone better, but when you are open to growth and development, that can only be a good thing! No one was born a trainer! It is something you work on and strengthen over the years, with each experience getting better and better.

What do I mean about leading with the heart? We'll look at it in more detail, in the next chapter. In fact, we will learn all about the E-Factor!

Ahhh! The Big Day Is Here!

"Doubt can motivate you, so don't be afraid of it. Confidence and doubt are at two ends of the scale, and you need both. They balance each other out." – Barbra Streisand

Chapter 6 Reflections...

Chapter 7

The E-Factor!

In the last chapter, I said to lead with your heart! What does that mean exactly? I'm not saying you need to be best friends with everyone and hang out every night, sharing stories of your childhood woes (although I am pretty sure I did that in Chapter 1). When you lead with the heart, you are focused on the individuals you are teaching, not on yourself. You see the stage as a position of power for the purpose to serve, not to impress. This isn't about you! We spoke about the trainer as a superhero. Superheroes don't help others so that they will go on and on about how wonderful they are. That may be a side effect of it but not the purpose of why they do it. The goal is to strengthen the bond you have begun to build with them. When you lead with your heart, you show them how important they are to you, and what you are willing to do to take them on this journey.

Participants will be watching you as a model. If you are talking to your assistant during a presentation, then you are sending a message that what the presenter is sharing is not important. Participants lose faith and respect in who you are. Communication, whether it is verbal or non-verbal, is critical to your success as a trainer. Whether it is your stance, your expression, or your tone of voice, the participants will make note of what you are saying through it.

Nonverbal communication refers to the process of sending and receiving messages without words. Refer to the chart below for some examples of both positive and negative non-verbal behaviours.

Areas of Focus	Positive	Negative
Facial expressions and eye gaze	Smiling, eye contact, happy, excited, relaxed face, nodding	Rolling of the eyes, bored look, looking distracted, lack of eye contact, angry, disgusted, disappointed, pursed lips, shaking of head, intense staring
Gestures and touch	Waving, thumbs up, pat on the back, high five, handshake	Clenched fists, looking at watch or phone, repeated or excessive gestures
Body language/posture	Standing upright, leaning in (but respecting personal space), open posture, facing the audience, standing to greet someone	Leaning away, poor or closed posture – slouching, hands on hips, arms crossed, fidgeting with hands, tapping of fingers, facing away from the audience
Spoken communication	Tone is animated	Low voice, monotonous
Appearance	Professional	Unprofessionally dressed (e.g., jeans and a t-shirt)

I'm sure you can think of a speaker who had a negative non-verbal behaviour. Sometimes you don't even notice until someone points it out. Some of these may overlap depending on the circumstances. For example, a thumbs up may be a positive sign in some parts of the world, but in others, it may be a bit offensive (another reason to be aware of who your audience is). Smiling is another example of being inappropriate if done at the wrong time. I know of at least one person who laughs when they see someone get hurt. (I know, it sounds strange, but they don't mean it. It just comes out!) This is by no means a comprehensive list but is a reminder that we are communicating with the audience even when we are not speaking out loud. I remember one trainer I had that had this look about him that was intimidating. Sure, he smiled as we walked in initially, but as the day went on, he had this air about him that almost made you fearful of going up to him to talk. It didn't help that during the session, he looked irritated at some of the comments or questions made by the participants. It doesn't take much for people to focus on the negative non-verbal behaviour, even if there are positive ones.

Then there are those trainers that look so bored. You see them constantly looking at their watch. I'm sure you must have had one of those. I know I have! You almost want to shout out, "Could you at least pretend you want to be here with us!"

Consider yourself as the captain of a ship. The audience will be watching and following your lead. If you honour them by showing them that you know what you are doing and talking about (confidence), and guide them to where they need to be (with patience and care), they will listen. If, however, you let your ego take control, and you don't respect what they bring to the table (and show your irritation), they could just as easily start a mutiny!

When you are out there as a trainer, you have a responsibility to do your best to ensure that the outcomes of the session are met. These are simple enough as they were determined as you were planning the session. However, as part of your journey, it is important to know why you are doing this. Is it for the fame or fortune, or is it for the opportunity to give back? Whether you are planning, preparing, or presenting, what are your goals? How will you gauge your success? When you are out there, you are leading the participants, guiding them as a mentor, and facilitating their journey. This is a big responsibility and should not be taken lightly.

What are your priorities as a leader? Is it important for you to be...?

- **Ethical?**
- **Engaging?**
- **Effective?**

To me, these are factors that create an **exemplary leader**. Let's break them down further to see if this is the kind of leader you are, or are working toward.

As an ethical leader, you set an example for others. Your actions and interactions are based on what you value as part of your beliefs. You embody ethics and values, such as respect, honesty, and empathy. You look for the good in others and encourage them to grow and develop, with your support along the way. Your interactions are always authentic and respectful of others. You take the time to get to know them individually, and you listen attentively when they speak. You make a point to understand the viewpoints of others and are transparent in all that you do.

As an engaging leader, you are ambitious, and you

maximize the potential of others. You build community by creating trusting relationships in which you show qualities of trust and respect. You bring a sense of energy to all that you do, which draws others to your side. Your positive attitude is contagious and draws others to you. You nurture an ethos of care, which others value, and through this, they are empowered.

As an effective leader, you get the job done, but not at the expense of others. Your care for others will always be a factor in what you do. You bring others along with you, never trampling them to get ahead. When requests are made of you, you respond in a timely manner; and if you can't, you inform them without delay, and you propose an alternative, which you stick to. You understand the importance of balance (not just for yourself but also for your team), and you do what it takes to build a team around you that stays energized. Together, you achieve a vision that inspires others.

As you can tell, these 3 characteristics are essential. As an exemplary leader, you empower others by creating an ethos of community. You model ethics in your actions and interactions. Your teams collaborate well together, harnessing innovation and creativity. They feel valued, and all achievements are acknowledged, but more importantly, they are also celebrated, not only by you but by your whole team.

Think about your favourite trainers. Did they exhibit these characteristics? If you want to build credibility as a trainer, you need to know what you stand for. What is important to you? Are there other characteristics that you would add to the list above? As a trainer who embodies exemplary leadership, imagine what you can achieve through your sessions. Imagine the transformation that can take place!

When I think of some of the leaders I have encountered over the years, I have had quite the range. Admittedly, I have had some that I wish had been more transparent. They may have said all the right things, but this didn't translate into their actions. It becomes really difficult to follow, learn from, or even listen to someone who doesn't walk the talk. I was never sure if they really meant what they were saying. Unfortunately, this then becomes a part of their branding.

I have also come across trainers that were confident but never afraid to ask for my thoughts and my help. When they were successful, they highlighted me and my colleagues, and what we had brought to the table. When you understand that your successes are not your own but those of the team you nurtured and mentored, you are branded as an exemplary leader.

Take a moment to reflect on how you want to be branded. Do you want to be seen as an exemplary leader? Do you want others to flock to your sessions because they know they will not only get meaningful training, but it will be done by someone who truly cares for the growth and development of others? They want to be trained by someone who will go out of their way to create a session that will engage, excite, and energize them. That's what happens when you lead from the heart!

I remember reading about this one pair of facilitators of a training session. Trainer A (let's call him Gabriel) was seasoned and knowledgeable. Trainer B (let's call her Jenna) was new and still learning the ropes. Gabriel was supposed to do the first 2 days of the training, and then Jenna would do the last 2 days. Gabriel knew a lot about the material they were going to be training on, which is why he always did the training. As Jenna sat there observing him (trying to learn as much as she could from the expert), she was surprised at what she saw. Gabriel's style was very dry, including his humour. He had very little participation from the audience, but when he did ask questions, he either didn't give them enough time to respond, or he responded to their answers by giving them what he called the *right* answers. He came off as arrogant and self-centred, not to mention that he was boring. By the time Jenna came to do her section of the training, the group had thinned out considerably, and although she tried to engage the participants, they had mentally checked out by that time.

The E-Factor!

As a trainer, you have an incredible opportunity to make a difference. You can truly transform individuals. BUT, in addition to preparing ahead of time, you need to go in with the right attitude. You must see your role in helping others, in serving them! When you go in there and lead with your heart, you are unstoppable! Being aware of how you come across to others is important, so be mindful of both your verbal and your non-verbal communication.

In an earlier chapter, you looked at what you thought was important in a trainer. How many of those qualities do you embody? What about the list above, on what it takes to be an exemplary leader? What do you still need to work on? Look, no one is automatically all of those things. (Yes, even me! We all have areas that we want to strengthen.) This will take time, but now is the time to start. If, however, you have convinced yourself that you already do all of these things, I am truly impressed. However, just to be sure that you are as good as you think you are, take a look at the evaluations you have received in the past. What were the participants saying about you, the facilitator? In their feedback, did they make note of how effective you were? Did they speak about how you made them feel? I know that it's not always easy, and I'm not going to pretend that there won't be days when you just want to shake your head at something that happened in your session. There WILL be days like that. How you respond will be a true testament to the kind of leader you are. How do you currently respond to times like this? More importantly, how will you respond to it from now on? Take a moment to reflect on it, and write your thoughts at the end of the chapter. Remember that this is a journey, and there is always room to grow (ahh, intellectual humility).

You may be thinking that most of these recommendations are for in-person sessions. What would you do if you didn't have the budget for that? Stay tuned for some suggestions in the next chapter!

"Strive not to be a success, but rather to be of value."
– Albert Einstein

Chapter 7 Reflections…

Chapter 8

No Budget? Are You Kidding? Now What Do I Do?

It's not always easy to find the budget for an in-person training. Sometimes it may even be a time factor. As mentioned earlier, in Chapter 4, there are other ways you can do the training.

Some of the alternatives include:

- **E-Learning modules**
- **Self-study modules**
- **Virtual training**

Let's break these down and see what you need to consider for these other options. Some of the considerations we have already covered may still be applied.

E-Learning modules are modules that are available online for participants to engage in. They can be available all at once, or it can be set up so that once a module is completed, the next level is made available. There are various components that are embedded in these modules. Initially, there may be a pre-assessment done to see the level of understanding the participant currently has of the topic to be trained in. After this, the modules that are relevant would be assigned to the participant.

If you choose this option, you would start off by creating learning outcomes (similar to any kind of training that is taken on). You would prepare assigned readings, as well as writing assignments. Having audio and video recording options can break up the monotony of reading, so consider those as well. There could also be various activities the participants could do to ensure they understand the content that is being covered. These can be mix and match, fill in the blanks, or explain what you would do in a particular scenario. Some of these can be self-checking activities, which really helps. You can even ask participants to post on discussion forums, and to respond to the posts of others. At the end of each module, you would require participants to complete an assessment in the form of an online quiz or test, and depending on the kind of questions you ask, they could get their mark right away. This assessment would measure how well the participant met the outcomes of the module.

Although creating the content of the modules may not be too difficult, ensuring that it works in an e-Learning format can require more technical expertise (not only for creating the online platform for this module, but also for the creation of the activities, and awareness of how to manage the site). In addition, you will need to have access to and follow up with the responses of the participants.

E-Learning modules can allow for participants to go at their own pace, unless timelines have been set by you. When participants are required to complete the components by certain timelines, it encourages participants to engage in discussion forums with other participants who are doing the module at the same time. You will need to moderate the forum to ensure that the comments are appropriate and meaningful. In addition to having access to a computer, the internet, and the portal where they can log on to access the module, the participant may need to be shown how to maneuver the site.

Self-study modules are very similar to e-Learning modules, but without the need to go online. Materials are provided to the participant, who then takes their time to complete some form of a handbook, where responses to the readings are embedded. Although this works for those that don't have access to the internet, this module doesn't allow for dialogue and engagement with others. Once the participant has completed the module, they can then submit their handbook to you, to be checked for understanding.

Virtual training incorporates elements of the in-person training by ensuring participants can see you, and depending on how you set it up, they can also see other participants who are logged on and are using their webcams as well. You can present the material by sharing your screen. You can play audio and video recordings, as well as ask participants to respond to online polls. Participants can also engage in discussions through the chat group, as well as orally, at your discretion. This format works really well for bringing together participants who live in different locations, but all need the same training. Some platforms even include break out rooms in which participants can be assigned to in case you need to divide the group up.

Ensuring participants are following what you are teaching (as opposed to looking at cat videos, catching up on emails, or on social media), can be a huge challenge. Not many people know this, but some platforms for webinars create reports that you can access post event, that show what percentage of people were actually looking at the presentation (i.e. they weren't multi-tasking by looking at other tabs on their computer). Admittedly, I have been guilty of doing that (at least prior to knowing about this feature!). Unfortunately, depending on the time you have scheduled the training, you may find it quite challenging to get people to respond to your questions, so having a colleague on the webinar to break the ice and get the ball rolling is a great way to deal with that.

There are several ways you can increase your chances of having participants pay attention to you (and not get distracted by other tasks).

1. Have a co-presenter do it with you. This can really liven up the training, as they won't be listening to the same voice the whole time.
2. Leaving your webcam on can allow participants to connect with you (at least for the beginning and end portion).
3. Start off with a hook. It could be a powerful story, or a myth you want to debunk.
4. Offer something free if they stay until the end. This can be a free pdf, or a draw for a free product, like a book.
5. Provide opportunities for them to engage in activities, like polling or playing an online game, where they are competing with others that are present.
6. Switch it up by showing them something related but in a different format (e.g. a video clip or an image that poses a question).
7. Keep it short (limit it to 30–45 minutes). It's hard to pay attention to a really long webinar.

8. Set aside a time for Q and A at the end. Participants want an opportunity to be heard and validated. This is a perfect opportunity for that.

Pre-recording your training is another option that provides you with flexibility in ensuring you have the best version out there. However, this doesn't allow for the meaningful engagement that can take place when doing it live. You can also record a live session and then make it available for those that missed it. Depending on the platform you use for the webinar, you can also set it up so anyone that watches the recording has to register to get access to it. This way, you can track who watched it. Just be aware that registering for it doesn't mean that they actually watched the whole recording.

Although budget is a major determinant of what format would work best, sometimes the topic will only allow for a certain format of training. At other times, having access to the internet may be an issue. Regardless of which one you choose, remember that quality is essential.

Quality of the training materials is important, but so is the way it is presented. Even if you are choosing to do a self-study module, remember to make it visually appealing so that as participants are going through it, they are excited (not always easy). Choose short but fascinating readings that are focused on the topic. If you choose to do an e-Learning module, have video recordings of real people that are relatable and tug at the emotions of the participants. Do whatever it takes to ensure that the participants will be engaged and excited to be learning about the topic.

The quality of your interactions with the participants will also be just as important. Respond to questions in a timely manner. Offer FAQs to help them. Provide the necessary training ahead of them completing the modules, so they feel confident prior to starting. Give participants advance notice of important dates to keep in mind. No one likes to be told last minute about an upcoming assignment or webinar.

Whatever format you choose to use, remember to provide follow-up and encouragement so participants feel you are vested in them. When they complete a module or the training, acknowledge it, and ensure you hand out a certificate at the end. Having it framed and presenting it in front of their peers can be a really nice way to show how much you value the time they put in to complete the training. Another great way to ensure they find value in it is to provide them with job aids (e.g. checklists or infographics) that they can refer to and use when they are finished with the training.

Now that it's done, what now? How do you know if you truly accomplished what you hoped to do? Check out the next chapter to find out!

"The only thing worse than training your employees and having them leave, is not training them and having them stay." – Henry Ford

Chapter 8 Reflections...

Chapter 9

I'm So Glad It's Done, But How Did I Do?

Waiting to hear how the training was perceived can be nerve-wracking! Luckily, for the in-person sessions at least, you can chat with participants during the breaks to get a feel of how they are finding the training so far. It often helps to have someone you know as a participant that will give you honest feedback. Usually, you can tell by the reaction of the audience as to whether they are enjoying it, but this doesn't always mean that the outcomes are being met.

The same can be said for live webinars. You can send a private message to someone you know to ask them how they think it is going. I find having a colleague present for webinars can be really helpful, especially to take care of any technical issues, respond to those that need help via the chat box, as well as to tell you if you need to speak up. If you want to know how the self-study module will be perceived, why not test it out by asking someone to try it prior to sharing it with others? You can then adjust it based on their feedback.

Evaluation forms are an essential component for getting feedback. However, there are some considerations you need to think through prior to using them. First, what is the purpose of the evaluation? What data do you want to collect? Second, who will look at the data? Third, what would be the best format for it, and how will it be administered? Fourth, who will be assigned to do the various tasks (e.g., creating the form, analyzing the data, etc.)? Once that has been figured out, you can start to flush out the details.

As mentioned earlier, evaluations can be handed out in advance (at the start of an in-person training), and participants can be reminded to fill it out throughout the day. I usually try to have time built into the training at the end, and then that becomes their exit ticket as they walk out the door! You can then see their input right away, which is a huge perk.

I'm So Glad It's Done, But How Did I Do?

For other training formats, it's best to send the link within 24 hours of the training, so their feedback would still be fresh on their minds. Some webinar platforms even include the option of sending a follow-up email with a survey link to encourage participants to complete it right away. Note that this option should be chosen prior to setting up the registration, as it may be harder to set up after the fact.

When deciding on the kinds of questions to ask, you will need to know if you want to have a rating scale (e.g., Strongly Agree, Agree, Disagree, and Strongly Disagree), open ended questions, multiple choice, etc. If the questions apply to certain participants and not all, then you may also need to include N/A (not applicable) as an option. Below, you will find some suggested headings (depending on the format your training takes), along with sample questions (Q) and statements (S) that can be used with ranges.

Content of the Training

Q: How well did the content of the session meet the objectives of the training?
Q: What is one thing you intend to use in your role as a result of this training?
S: I will be able to use this learning right away in my role.
S: I found the training increased my understanding of the topic covered.
S: I found the information presented to be relevant and practical for my role.

Trainer Effectiveness

Q: How engaging was the main presenter?
Q: How knowledgeable did you find the trainer to be on this topic?
S: I felt the trainer created a comfortable learning environment.
S: I felt supported by the trainer.
S: The activities led by the trainer were appropriate and engaging.

Learning Platform

Q: How would you rate the ability to connect with your peers on this platform?
Q: How would you rate the overall feel and look of the platform?
S: I felt the learning platform for the training was easy to navigate.

Materials for Training

S: I felt the materials and resources for the training were relevant and helpful.
S: The overall look and feel of the materials were visually appealing.
S: The activities in the materials were appropriate and engaging.

I'm So Glad It's Done, But How Did I Do?

Overall Feedback:

Q: What would have made the training even more effective?
Q: What additional content would you like to see added to the training?
Q: How likely are you to recommend others to take this training?
Q: Please share any additional comments you may have.
S: The length of the training was appropriate.
S: The format of the training worked well.

You want to be able to keep the evaluation short and sweet but at the same time receive meaningful feedback. Notice that I didn't focus on the venue, food, etc. Don't worry; if they felt strongly about it, they will find a place to share that. As you don't want to have too long of a form, you want to select the questions that will give you the feedback you need in order to see if the training was successful in meeting its objectives.

For the purposes of analysis, having ratings makes it much easier. It also helps to cluster questions based on their theme. Be mindful of the participants as questions are created. Ensure they are not biased in any way, and that the questions are clear and precise. Once the form has been created, have someone proofread it to ensure there are no errors.

Although you may want to provide a link to the form (it saves a lot of paper!), some participants may prefer a hard copy to write their feedback on. Just ensure you have help to enter the data if there is a large number who choose to do that. There are several options for online creation of feedback forms. Choose the one that works best for you.

Hard copies are great because you get to see the feedback right away, but it can be hard to see patterns and do a proper analysis until they have been entered into the computer. While waiting for the feedback, there are some things you can do to gauge how it went. Talk to the participants to see how they found the session. As I said earlier, you should be able to see throughout the session as to how engaged they are. Listen to the conversations taking place. Participants will come up to you personally and tell you if they found it helpful. Feel the energy of the room. Is there a buzz, or do you feel like people are just anxious to leave? Mind you, if the training has been a few days, people may want to leave right away, not because they didn't find value but because they are probably drained. Just remember to thank them for coming as they are walking out (and perhaps they can be handed a certificate as they are leaving)!

You can also reach out to the person who asked you to do the training. Ask them what they are hearing from the participants. Believe me, they will be honest, especially if they paid for it!

When you finally do read the comments, be open to the feedback. You can't please everyone! You're bound to have at least a few that will leave you curious as to how they could even say what they did. As you look through the feedback, look for patterns. What are you noticing? What are areas of strength of the training, and what needs to be improved upon for the next time?

You may be asked to compile a report, post training. It is generally best to keep it concise; try not to get too bogged down with the details (especially when it comes to the feedback). The following are suggestions as to what can be included in the report:

- Title of training, location (if applicable), date and name of facilitator
- Purpose of training and objectives
- Number of participants and their background
- Outline of the training (including topics covered and instructional activities)
- Key findings
- Recommendations for future
- Appendix (supporting documentation, such as agenda, slides, etc.)

Wherever you see a good fit, acknowledge the people who were critical to the implementation of the training. These individuals should be recognized in person as well as in the report. We know that these initiatives can't be done by a single individual. By showing you appreciate the team, you send a strong message that you value their contributions, and this can go a long way in creating a collaborative and unified team. Think of the E-factor and the kind of leader you are!

The truth is that there are probably many people that supported it, from the staff at the venue, to the IT technician, to the food vendor, your family at home, your boss that encouraged you, and the list goes on. Take a moment to thank them too! You may even want to send a follow-up email to the participants to thank them for their engagement, and if you are able to support them, that would be a good opportunity to do a follow-up with them. Most times, trainings are done as a one-off, and you don't get to see the return on investment, post session. Were they able to transfer their knowledge once they got back into the field? At the end of the day, that is the most critical component, and yet very little time is spent on that, partially because it is hard to measure that impact. In case you do have an opportunity to do this, it would be important to include that in the report.

Personally, I am not a huge fan of reports. I generally find that creating a report can take a long time, and although it may be looked at by one or two individuals, it then gets filed away and is rarely looked at again. One way to ensure that it is used in a meaningful manner is to take some time to reflect on the feedback. With your team, make a list of what changes are essential (but be willing to explain why you wouldn't make a particular change). As you look at this list, reflect on what is doable (some may even be quick fixes), what is necessary (because the outcome would be beneficial), and the cost involved (that's probably the first question that is asked by the boss). It's not always easy to acknowledge things you did wrong, but now is not the time for justifying why you did certain things! Come up with ideas (or even acknowledge that you need to spend time on finding a solution for certain changes) that will help take the training to the next level. Once this is done, come up with an action plan based on this list, a timeline in which it will be done, and assign people to the tasks.

There is a greater chance that it will be done if it is done right away. (Believe me, procrastination is something that runs in the family!) This way, the next time this training is used, it already has the changes embedded in it. In fact, the next time you do the training, acknowledge to the participants that based on the feedback that was received, several changes have been made. When participants know that their voice matters, they feel valued and are more likely to complete the feedback form when it is time.

Wondering what's next on your horizon? Will it be a bed of roses? Turn to the next chapter to see what lies ahead!

"Do the one thing you think you cannot do. Fail at it. Try again. Do better the second time. The only people who never tumble are those who never mount the high wire. This is your moment. Own it." – Oprah Winfrey

Chapter 9 Reflections…

Chapter 10

Hey, I Can Do This!

This has been quite the journey! You now have the tools to be a successful trainer! There is no turning back now as you move to the next chapter in your life! Whether you seek to be a more confident public speaker, a more powerful trainer, or even an engaging educator, I know you can do it! Half the battle is knowing what to do. We have gone through this journey together, from start to finish, and you know everything you need to be a superhero and help transform lives.

I'm not going to lie to you. There will be those who will try to shut you down. They will give you a million reasons why you can't do this, but you now know how wrong they are. How do you know? You have been reflecting at the end of each chapter on how you can grow in this journey. If you haven't, you have been thinking about it in your head; and don't worry, you can still go back and fill it out. Also, this book can be used as a reference at any time. If you are in the planning stage, look at the section that walks you through it. If you need to know what to focus on for evaluation, turn to that section. It doesn't end there! For additional support, just turn to my website for more tools to support you.

Besides believing in yourself (which I can't emphasize enough!), you will need to practice and practice and practice! As I began my own journey as a trainer, my colleagues and I were often given opportunities to speak in front of an audience. For some reason, they usually had reasons why they couldn't do it, and so it would fall on me to do it, and so I did. I wasn't always a strong speaker, but being a people person, I liked to be out there, talking to others (yes, this is the girl who was too shy to raise her hand in class). The more I did these sessions, the more comfortable and confident I became. Those same colleagues were joking the other day about how I wouldn't have been here had it not been for them! True enough! I am grateful for every opportunity I had to practice!

Like mine, your journey may not always be easy, but if you follow the suggestions in this book, you will become more comfortable, more confident, and more creative in the way you do your training. Remember to celebrate every step of the way, even if in your mind they were tiny successes. Each one adds on to the next. Even when you have challenges, that is still okay, because you will learn from it; and the next time, you will crush it! That is why I chose that for the title. What does it mean to crush it? It means to succeed beyond expectations. That's what is going to happen here. It's true that you have to want it, and I believe you do! You just have to believe in yourself!

You are special. No one is like you. Integrate who you are, into your training (remember that someone actually wrote *dodging potholes* as one of their skillsets in their resume). Every time someone gives you an opportunity to speak in front of a group, thank them! They gave you a platform for you to practice and strengthen your skills. If you lead with the heart, you will find the energy, the drive, and the passion to do it well. Just remember your purpose. What is it you want to achieve? Is it about the money and the job, or is it about serving others? When we do things from the heart, we are infused with this energy that propels us forward. When we help others, we help ourselves.

This journey you are on is on-going. Continue to find opportunities to observe other speakers, and take notes. I still do that! Every opportunity I get, I try to learn from those around me. I still remember to think about what *gem* I can walk away with. When you are open to growth and development, you see that the universe is bountiful in its gifts to you. It's important that we realize that this is a journey of life-long learning, and that if we use it to help others, we will find peace within ourselves. I know that it does come off sounding somewhat corny, but I truly believe this!

I spoke about how important it is to observe others, but it is equally important to find someone that you can trust to observe you and help you see your strengths and areas of growth while you are on this journey. Choose someone who you respect and that you know will not be making this all about them. This is about your growth. Each time you do a session, have a goal that you want to work toward. Share this goal with them, and tell them what you would like for them to look for. For example, if you want to work on your relationship building with the participants, you may want to ask your colleague to note how often you go and talk to participants, and to note examples of verbal and non-verbal communication, both on and off stage. (Go over this prior to the session so you are both on the same page as to what that will look like.) You decide what it is you want to work on, based on the areas that you need to develop. You could even ask them to video tape you. I remember the first time I watched a recording of myself facilitating. I have to admit, I was a bit embarrassed, but at the end of the day, I picked up on a few habits that I knew I needed to change.

If you are co-facilitating a session with someone, make sure you debrief at the end of it. You may want to ask them if there is something you could work on for the next time you do it together. After one particular session, when reflecting with my colleague, I remember being told that I had interrupted them and then took over when they were supposed to speak. Admittedly, that probably happened more than once. It was hard to hear and, at the time, I got a bit defensive. However, when I reflected on it, they were right; I did do that. I realized that it was because I was so excited to share something that I just blurted it out and kept going. I was not honouring my colleague by doing this, and I knew I had to consciously ensure it didn't happen again. My colleague was very gracious, and had they not told me what I was doing, I can only imagine the resentment that would have built up. It's not easy co-facilitating with someone, but setting ground rules from the beginning helps. When I facilitate with someone, one of the things we discuss is whether they are open to someone stepping in with a comment while they are doing their portion (within reason, not all the time). Some are and some aren't. Either way, it's good to know in advance. In case there is something you want to bring up, determine if it is important for the participants to know, and if it can wait until you are doing your portion of the training. Most of the time, it can usually wait.

As you can tell, I have had a lot of learnings on my journey to be a successful trainer. It takes time, patience, drive, and heart! It's a never-ending journey, but it is very fulfilling. I truly believe that. I was speaking to a colleague the other day, and she told me how proud she was of me for putting all of my knowledge out there for others to gain from my experiences. This is what drives me. It's not about the compliments (although, hey, we all like to hear acknowledgements, don't we?), but it's about knowing you can help others. I have also had many mentors along the way, to guide me. In addition, I have had many opportunities that I wouldn't have had if I had been anywhere else. This is when I am reminded that it is my responsibility to give back.

Enough about me—let's focus on your next steps! You may want to go out there and find a mentor if you don't already have one. Think of someone you feel has the E-factor, who helps others transform their lives. Observe them, ask them questions, and learn as much as you can from them. You may even want to video tape them (a reminder to ask for their permission) or watch a recording if there is one. Make note of their verbal and non-verbal communication. Listen to how they frame things, and what kinds of activities they do. Make sure you document everything!

Next, you need to find opportunities to practice. In some cases, you will have opportunities through your role. If not, think about how you can give back in your community, where you live. Is there a way you can get involved in something you feel passionate or knowledgeable about? Go out there and find opportunities. You will have the most impact when it is something you care about! If you need the boost, find a co-facilitator that you feel comfortable with.

Once you have secured one, go step-by-step through the different chapters to ensure you are not forgetting anything (from marketing to storyboarding to the actual implementation). If you have a partner, ensure they are part of this process. If possible, have someone videotape it. I know it won't be easy to watch, but I promise you will learn a lot!

When it is done, celebrate! Admittedly, there have been a few times when I felt a bit down after completing a session (perhaps the attendance was low, or there were some major technical challenges). That's when I take a deep breath and make note of what went well and what areas I need to address next time. There have also been times when I have been on a natural high at the end of a session, and it can last for a few days! That's when I hear from the participants about how much they valued the training, about the "aha" moment they had, or how they can't wait to implement something I showed them! That's when I know it was all worth it; and although I am mentally and physically exhausted, I feel this energy that I truly have no idea where it came from. This is when I know my purpose. This is why

Crushing It On Stage

I do it. I truly hope that this is what you will experience as a trainer once you go out there and show the world what you've got. You and I may not have the same style of doing things, and hopefully your jokes aren't as lame as mine. One thing I know for sure is that when you lead with your heart, you can accomplish anything. You can crush it! I look forward to hearing all about it when you do!

Hey, I Can Do This!

"Satisfaction lies in the effort, not in the attainment. Full effort is full victory." – Mahatma Gandhi

Chapter 10 Reflections...

About the Author

Fauzia Moorani is an award-winning author, trainer, certified teacher, and motivational speaker who loves to crack jokes, despite her family's insistence that she isn't very funny.

Having been in the business of adult training for over 15 years, she continues to find passion in empowering others to be the best in the field of education and training as a whole.

Fauzia currently lives in Toronto, Canada, but is available for delivering keynote presentations to audiences around the world. For rates and availability, please contact the author directly at fauzia@crushingitonstage.com.

To order more books, please visit CrushingItOnStage.com. Finally, if you have been inspired by this book, the best thing you could do is to pass that on and be a wonderful role model for others. This world needs more superheroes who lead with the heart!

www.ingramcontent.com/pod-product-compliance
Lightning Source LLC
Chambersburg PA
CBHW070919160426
43193CB00011B/1527